RETHINKING
—THE—
SYNOPTIC
PROBLEM

Edited by
David Alan Black
and David R. Beck

Baker Academic
A Division of Baker Book House Co
Grand Rapids, Michigan 49516

Published by Baker Academic
a division of Baker Book House Company
P.O. Box 6287, Grand Rapids, MI 49516-6287

Printed in the United States of America

Library of Congress Cataloging-in-Publication Data

Rethinking the synoptic problem / edited by David Alan Black and David R. Beck.
    p.   cm.
Includes bibliographical references and index.
ISBN 0-8010-2281-9 (paper)
    1. Bible. N.T. Gospels—Criticism, interpretation, etc. I. Black, David Alan, 1952– II. Beck, David R.
BS2555.2 .R47   2001
226'.066—dc21   2001035448

For information about Baker Academic, visit our web site:
www.bakerbooks.com/academic

RETHINKING
—THE—
SYNOPTIC
PROBLEM

To Professor D. Moody Smith
and to the memory of Professor Bo Reicke

CONTENTS

ABBREVIATIONS

AB	Anchor Bible
ABD	*Anchor Bible Dictionary.* Ed. D. N. Freeman. 6 vols. New York, 1992
ABRL	Anchor Bible Reference Library
ANRW	*Aufstieg und Niedergang der römischen Welt: Geschichte und Kultur Roms im Spiegel der neueren Forschung.* Ed. H. Temporini and W. Haase. Berlin, 1972–
BETL	Bibliotheca ephemeridum theologicarum lovaniensium
Bib	*Biblica*
BJS	Brown Judaic Studies
BZ	*Biblische Zeitschrift*
CBQ	*Catholic Biblical Quarterly*
CBQMS	Catholic Biblical Quarterly Monograph Series
CTR	*Criswell Theological Review*
DJG	*Dictionary of Jesus and the Gospels.* Ed. J. B. Green and S. McKnight. Downers Grove, Ill., 1992
EuroJTh	*European Journal of Theology*
ETL	*Ephemerides theologicae lovanienses*
ETS	Erfurter theologische Studien
FB	Forschung zur Bibel
GTA	Göttinger theologischer Arbeiten
ICC	International Critical Commentary
JBL	*Journal of Biblical Literature*
JSNT	*Journal for the Study of the New Testament*

JSNTSup	Journal for the Study of the New Testament: Supplement Series
JSOTMan	Journal for the Study of the Old Testament Manuals
JTS	*Journal of Theological Studies*
MSJ	*Master's Seminary Journal*
NGS	New Gospel Studies
NIGTC	New International Greek Testament Commentary
NovT	*Novum Testamentum*
NovTSup	Novum Testamentum Supplements
NTAbh	Neutestamentliche Abhandlungen
NTS	*New Testament Studies*
NTTS	New Testament Tools and Studies
PSB	*Princeton Seminary Bulletin*
QC	*Qumran Chronicle*
RHPR	*Revue d'histoire et de philosophie religieuses*
SAC	Studies in Antiquity and Christianity
SBLDS	Society of Biblical Literature Dissertation Series
SBLMS	Society of Biblical Literature Monograph Series
SBLSCS	Society of Biblical Literature Septuagint and Cognate Studies
SNTSMS	Society for New Testament Studies Monograph Series
SNTW	Studies of the New Testament and Its World
TJ	*Trinity Journal*
TUMSR	Trinity University Monograph Series in Religion
WBC	Word Biblical Commentary
WMANT	Wissenschaftliche Monographien zum Alten und Neuen Testament
WTJ	*Westminster Theological Journal*
WUNT	Wissenschaftliche Untersuchungen zum Alten und Neuen Testament
ZNW	*Zeitschrift für die neutestamentliche Wissenschaft*
ZWB	Zürcher Werkkommentare zur Bibel

INTRODUCTION

DAVID ALAN BLACK AND DAVID R. BECK

The adjective "synoptic" has been used since the time of J. J. Griesbach (ca. 1790) to describe the first three canonical gospels—Matthew, Mark, and Luke. It is derived from the fact that these three Gospels can be arranged and harmonized section by section so as to allow the eye to see at a glance numerous passages that are common to them all, as well as portions that are peculiar to only two, or even one, of them. The interconnections between the Synoptic Gospels are not, however, only those of close resemblances but also those of striking differences, for when compared minutely, the three records appear distinct as well as similar in language, arrangement, and detail. Even in those passages that indicate a close relationship between the three, minor differences continually appear, which can be fully appreciated only through a diligent study of the parallel passages in Greek.

These resemblances and differences that become evident upon a careful comparison of the Synoptic Gospels constitute a phenomenon unique in all of ancient literature. On the one hand, to most observers the resemblances seem too numerous and too striking to be explained on the basis of the hypothesis that the first three evangelists wrote independently of one another; and, on the other hand, the differences are at times so significant as to imply the use of different sources by the evangelists. Thus, both the harmony and the variety—the resem-

11

blances and the differences—between these three Gospels must be accounted for. This literary problem is known today as the Synoptic problem, and the discussion of the origin of the possible mutual relationships between the first three Gospels has been carried on with great vigor and ingenuity since the First World War.

Numerous attempts have been made to solve the Synoptic problem. The oral theory states that the similarities among the Gospels are attributable to the fact that all three Gospels draw from oral traditions deriving from the early Christian community. The amazing similarities between the Synoptic Gospels appear to stand as a strong testimony to the tenacity of these traditions. Advocates of this view include Tom Shepherd and John Wenham. For Augustine, the canonical order of the Gospels also indicated the order of composition: Matthew, Mark, Luke, John. This theory is thought to find some support in the statements of the early church fathers and has been presumed for much of church history. Modern advocates include John Chapman and B. C. Butler.

The most dominant proposed solution by far is the two-source hypothesis (also known as the Oxford hypothesis), which is so widely accepted today that it is being used for other fields of study, including textual criticism, form criticism, redaction criticism, and early church history. This hypothesis argues that Mark was the earliest of our Gospels and that Matthew and Luke drew on another source, usually designated as Q, for the non-Markan material they share. This has been the predominant hypothesis since B. H. Streeter's presentation of it in 1924, which itself summarized and refined decades of research on the Gospels. The four-source version of the hypothesis, Streeter's own contribution, adds two additional sources to account for the unique material in Matthew's and Luke's Gospels. Thus, in addition to Q, Matthew uses M (material unique to Matthew) and Luke employs L (material unique to Luke).

Perhaps the most carefully articulated challenge to the two-source hypothesis is that of William Farmer, who claims that Matthew was written first, that Luke used Matthew in preparing his Gospel, and that Mark conflated the two. This view, known as the two-Gospel hypothesis, would (if sustained) call into question many of the conclusions of twentieth-century Gospel research. Like the Augustinian theory, it claims to find support in the statements of the church fathers.

The editors of this volume have long been aware that these (and various other) solutions to the Synoptic problem comprise a lively topic of discussion among students, not least on the campus of Southeastern Seminary. Would it not be useful, we mused, if we could assemble in Wake Forest leading proponents of the various solutions and let them present their views so that students could make up their own minds? At the same time, could we not examine other disputed areas of New Testament criticism as well?

With President Patterson's enthusiastic support, it was decided to organize a New Testament symposium on Southeastern's campus. Dr. Black would be responsible for contacting prospective participants and for arranging the program, while Dr. Beck would handle the on-campus arrangements. No expense was to be spared in making our guests feel welcome. The visiting scholars would be housed in our comfortable guest cottages (the Manor and Lyon Houses), and meals would be taken at Magnolia Hill, the president's home. The speakers would be met personally at the airport and shuttled to and from campus. Finally, the campus bookstore would set up a special display of the participants' publications for sale in the foyer of Binkley Chapel, the venue for the symposium.

So it was that on April 6–7, 2000, some of the world's leading experts in the field of New Testament studies convened in Wake Forest to read papers and to engage in dialog with their colleagues. The conference, titled "Symposium on New Testament Studies: A Time for Reappraisal," was designed to expose students and other interested parties to the main positions held by New Testament scholars in three debated areas of research: the Synoptic problem, the authorship of Hebrews, and New Testament textual criticism. Each seminar included a keynote address laying out in broad terms the *status quaestionis* in the area under debate, three main papers, a response, and a panel discussion.

In his keynote address on the Synoptic problem, Craig Blomberg introduced the audience to the contemporary relevance of Synoptic studies and provided a perspective for understanding current and future issues. Following Dr. Blomberg's overview, Darrell Bock presented the evidence for and against

Q. According to Dr. Bock, the Q hypothesis derives its main strength from the broader explanation it provides for the entire relationship between all three Synoptic Gospels. Thus, for example, the existence of doublets in Matthew and Luke, which are shared by Mark, argues for the existence of the Q Gospel because they indicate places where material is paralleled from Mark and another source. Q would also account for much of the verbatim agreement between Matthew and Luke when they include sayings absent from Mark. The fact that the sayings are used in different ways or different contexts in Matthew and Luke is an indication of the freedom with which the editors could take material and mold it to their situations and needs.

The paper by Scot McKnight then followed. Dr. McKnight is an outspoken defender of the two-source hypothesis and presents what in his opinion are the strongest arguments in its favor. He shows how the two-source theory has earned its prominent place among scholars in view of the significant and cumulative force of the evidence (especially the linguistic argument). While the two-source theory is not perfect, Dr. McKnight argues that it best explains the Synoptic problem and that, in the end, there is still good reason to think that the Gospel of Mark is the middle document between Matthew and Luke and that the latter two evangelists made use of Q.

As noted above, the two-source theory has been increasingly challenged in the last several decades from a variety of standpoints. In 1964, William Farmer challenged the status quo by reintroducing a theory from the literary-dependence family. The two-Gospel hypothesis, formerly known as the Griesbach hypothesis, proposes that the Gospel of Matthew was the earliest Gospel, that the author of the Gospel of Luke used the Gospel of Matthew as a source, and that the author of the Gospel of Mark wrote using both the Gospels of Matthew and Luke as sources. This theory gained momentum in 1995 when the *New Interpreter's Bible* stated that Markan priority was "weak and inconclusive." Thus, following Dr. McKnight's paper, William Farmer offered a defense of the two-Gospel hypothesis and presented what he holds to be the most viable theory of Gospel origins. Dr. Farmer also made available to his co-panelists a detailed addendum to his paper as well as a number of books and essays devoted to the two-Gospel hypothesis.

Grant Osborne then read his response to his colleagues' papers, which was followed by a panel discussion that allowed the audience to pose questions to the scholars and that gave the scholars themselves an opportunity to engage in further dialog. The reaction to the Southeastern symposium was enthusiastic, with over four hundred registered guests in attendance for some or all of the conference. It is now our pleasure to make the papers on the Synoptic problem available to the reading public. The editors are well aware that the essays that follow have at least two significant omissions, for there are neither separate chapters nor substantive discussions devoted to either the independence theory or the Farrer hypothesis. The former theory denies any direct literary interdependence between the Synoptic Gospels, while the latter hypothesis (named for its seminal supporter, A. M. Farrer) argues that Mark was written first and was adopted by Matthew, and then both were used by Luke, thus dispensing with Q. Perhaps the organizers were remiss in not assigning separate contributions on these subjects, but when this symposium on the New Testament was being planned, it was decided to invite representatives of what were considered to be the leading alternative positions being proffered today, at least on this side of the Atlantic.

Deep appreciation goes to each person involved in the planning and production of this volume, most especially to the authors themselves. Additional thanks are extended to our research assistants, Chris Thompson and Andrew Neamtu, for cheerfully attending to a myriad of details; to our secretaries, Janet Hellard, Phyllis Jackson, and Phyllis Keith, for their assistance with registration and correspondence; to Davidson Press for underwriting a portion of the symposium expenses; to Jim Kinney and his staff at Baker Books for their meticulous care in the publishing of this book; and especially to President Patterson and Dean Bush of Southeastern Seminary for their support of the project from its inception. We dedicate this volume to Professor D. Moody Smith (for David Beck) and to the memory of Professor Bo Reicke (for David Black), who directed our doctoral programs and modeled for us a perfect blend of *humanitas* and *pietas* in New Testament scholarship. We also note with deep sadness the passing of Professor William Farmer as this book was going to press.

1

THE SYNOPTIC PROBLEM

Where We Stand at the Start
of a New Century

CRAIG L. BLOMBERG

In the early 1960s, a history of modern biblical scholarship claimed that the solution to the Synoptic problem was one of the few settled issues of recent criticism: Matthew and Luke each used Mark, along with a second, shorter source designated Q (from the German *Quelle* for "source") for the non-Markan material they shared.[1] Toward the end of the 1990s, some scholars virtually claimed that this two-source hypothesis had been disproved![2] In fact, neither claim was warranted, but there is

1. Stephen Neill, *The Interpretation of the New Testament 1861–1961* (London and New York: Oxford University Press, 1964), 339.
2. See, for example, Allan J. McNicol with David L. Dungan and David B. Peabody, *Beyond the Q Impasse: Luke's Use of Matthew* (Valley Forge, Pa.: Trinity, 1996), 318–19.

today considerably greater diversity of scholarly opinion than there was forty years ago. This paper surveys the landscape; subsequent presentations argue, in turn, for three different, specific solutions.

I begin with three disclaimers. First, I am not the most obvious choice of the four speakers on this topic to provide the broad overview. Three of us—Scot McKnight, Darrell Bock, and I—are peers. I had the privilege of going to seminary with Scot and to graduate school with Darrell. We have all studied and written widely on the Synoptic Gospels,[3] but none of us has committed an entire career to researching the Synoptic problem the way William Farmer has.[4] He could no doubt provide a far more nuanced overview of the state of the art, but I have been chosen for that task so that he can argue in detail for his preferred position, and because I may not be quite as strongly committed to any one perspective as are our other presenters.

Second, because this conference is occuring in an evangelical context, it is important to state up front that none of the major solutions to the Synoptic problem is inherently more or less compatible with historic Christian views of the inspiration and authority of Scripture. Nevertheless, certain versions of particular solutions clearly are less compatible, most notably when it is assumed, after determining directions of literary dependence among paralleled material, that unparalleled material can have come only from the Gospel writers' imaginations. But as I try to formulate a particular approach, I do so understanding that I am trying to determine how the Gospels' human authors wrote, in keeping with Luke's prologue that describes him functioning as would other historians or biographers of his day—relying on previously written sources, interviewing eyewitnesses, ordering and crafting his material to support his distinctive theological emphases, all for the sake of commending the truth of the Gospel (Luke 1:1–4). I simultaneously affirm that the results of my investigation will demonstrate how God superintended the process of cre-

---

3. See esp. Craig L. Blomberg, *Jesus and the Gospels: An Introduction and Survey* (Nashville: Broadman & Holman; Leicester: InterVarsity, 1998); Scot McKnight, *Interpreting the Synoptic Gospels* (Grand Rapids: Baker, 1988); Darrell L. Bock, *Luke*, 2 vols. (Grand Rapids: Baker, 1994–96).

4. William R. Farmer's pioneering work, *The Synoptic Problem* (New York and London: Macmillan, 1964), may still be his most important.

ating an inerrant Scripture that included exactly what he wanted it to include (2 Pet. 1:21), but that does not alter the actual contents of the texts of the Synoptics with which all interpreters, of whatever ideological perspective, must grapple. Thus, my survey must scan all major contributions to the topic, irrespective of the theological commitments of their proponents.

Third, I limit this survey to what has traditionally come under the rubric of the "Synoptic problem"—the question of the written sources of Matthew, Mark, and Luke, and the literary interrelationship of these three Gospels. The most recent history of the Synoptic problem, by David Dungan, casts its net far more widely, covering issues of textual criticism, canonization, and hermeneutics as well, demonstrating the interrelatedness of each of these three issues with source-critical questions.[5] It is a fascinating study that I highly commend, but I cannot hope in this short time to do anything as wide-ranging.

With this introduction, let us turn to the major solutions to the Synoptic problem. I discuss them in what I perceive to be a decreasing order of probability, which also roughly corresponds to a decreasing order of how commonly each is held. Obviously, not all of us agree that these two sequences match each other. Also I focus on the most recent and important work in each area, because the literature is voluminous and others have well documented earlier developments.[6]

The Four-Document Hypothesis

I have already alluded to the two-document hypothesis as the view that Matthew and Luke each used Mark and Q. In his classic presentation of this perspective in 1924, B. H. Streeter included two other documents: Matthew and Luke also relied on written sources, designated M and L respectively, for much of

5. David L. Dungan, *A History of the Synoptic Problem: The Canon, the Text, the Composition and the Interpretation of the Gospels*, ABRL (New York and London: Doubleday, 1999).

6. In addition to Dungan, *History*, and the previous historical surveys cited therein, see esp. the thorough bibliography by T. R. W. Longstaff and P. A. Thomas, *The Synoptic Problem: A Bibliography, 1716–1988*, NGS 4 (Macon, Ga.: Mercer University Press, 1988).

the nonparalleled material in each of their narratives.[7] We may look at each of these parts of the four-source hypothesis separately, again in decreasing order of probability and acceptance.

Markan Priority

Despite the alternatives soon to be mentioned, the vast majority of the introductions and surveys of the Gospels or of the life of Christ and the major commentaries on each of the Synoptics, along with studies more focused on individual themes or passages within those Gospels, all presuppose that Matthew and Luke each used Mark. I briefly list what I think are the nine most important reasons for this in my *Jesus and the Gospels:* (1) Mark frequently contains vivid touches, possibly the product of eyewitness testimony, that Matthew or Luke omit. (2) Matthew and Luke often seem to smooth out Mark's rougher grammar. (3) Matthew and Luke often omit potentially misleading details in Mark. (4) Mark is the shortest of the Synoptics, yet within individual pericopae he is consistently longer than Matthew or Luke, an unlikely result of later abbreviation. (5) Less than 10 percent of Mark is nonparalleled; why would Mark have written at all if longer, fuller treatments were already available and he had so little new to say? (6) Comparatively, Matthew and Luke rarely differ from Mark in the same way at the same time, whereas Mark and Matthew much more frequently agree with each other against Luke, as do Luke and Mark against Matthew. (7) Mark contains the highest incidence of Aramaisms among the Synoptics. (8) There seems to be no reason for Mark's omission of so much of Matthew and Luke that contains many of Jesus' most precious teachings, if Mark knew of them from a source. (9) When one assumes Markan priority, coherent patterns of redactional emphases emerge in ways that are not true on alternative models.[8] More detailed evangelical treatments of these and other points may be found in works by Robert Stein, Donald Guthrie, and Scot McKnight.[9] From other theological

7. B. H. Streeter, *The Four Gospels: A Study of Origins* (London and New York: Macmillan, 1924).

8. Blomberg, *Jesus and the Gospels*, 87–90.

9. Robert H. Stein, *The Synoptic Problem: An Introduction* (Grand Rapids: Baker, 1987), 29–157; Donald Guthrie, *New Testament Introduction*, rev. ed. (Leicester and Downers Grove, Ill.: InterVarsity), 136–208; Scot McKnight,

traditions, Joseph Fitzmyer and Christopher Tuckett are particularly thorough and persuasive in their presentations.[10]

Because Markan priority is so widely accepted, there are but
few detailed new works pursuing the question further. Nevertheless, we may mention six areas where progress in the last decade has been made. First, Maurice Casey has devoted an entire
book to the Aramaic sources of Mark.[11] Doubtless he has overstated his case. Several of his points depend on his somewhat
idiosyncratic and nontitular understanding of the Aramaic
background for "Son of man" or on his evolutionary hypothesis
of early Christianity that sees the historical Jesus as nothing
more than a Jewish prophet.[12] Still, the Aramaic substrata Casey discerns (e.g., in Mark 2:23–3:6 and 10:35–45) do suggest
sufficiently that Mark's Greek translation often renders Jesus'
words more literally than do Matthew or Luke.

Second, the young British evangelical Peter Head has published an important dissertation on the use of the christological
argument in solving the Synoptic problem. Arguing, contra
standard defenses of Markan priority, that Matthew and Luke
do not uniformly clear up potentially embarrassing or confusing details of Mark's presentation of Jesus, Head nevertheless
concludes that selected aspects of Matthew's Christology, particularly his use of the titles Teacher, Lord, Christ, and Son of
David, do make much more sense on the assumption that Matthew was using Mark rather than vice-versa.[13]

Third, David New has analyzed all of the quotations of the

"Source Criticism," in *Interpreting the New Testament*, ed. David A. Black and
David S. Dockery (Nashville: Broadman & Holman, 2001), 74–105.

10. Joseph A. Fitzmyer, "The Priority of Mark and the 'Q' Source in Luke," in
Jesus and Man's Hope, 2 vols. (Pittsburgh: Pittsburgh Theological Seminary,
1970), 2:131–70; Christopher M. Tuckett, *The Revival of the Griesbach Hypothesis*, SNTSMS 44 (Cambridge: Cambridge University Press, 1983).

11. Maurice Casey, *Aramaic Sources of Mark's Gospel*, SNTSMS 102 (Cambridge: Cambridge University Press, 1998).

12. Here Casey builds on his book-length treatment of both topics: *Son of
Man: The Interpretation and Influence of Daniel 7* (London: SPCK, 1980); idem,
*From Jewish Prophet to Gentile God: The Origins and Development of New Testa-
ment Christology* (Cambridge: James Clarke; Louisville: Westminster John
Knox, 1991).

13. Peter M. Head, *Christology and the Synoptic Problem: An Argument for
Markan Priority*, SNTSMS 94 (Cambridge: Cambridge University Press, 1997).

Old Testament in the Synoptics, of which Matthew by far includes the most. He compares them with Hebrew and Greek versions of the Old Testament, arguing that even Matthew's most distinctive, nonparalleled forms may reflect lesser-known versions of the Septuagint. Still, there is a difference between Matthew's paralleled and nonparalleled material that New believes can be accounted for only by Markan priority. If Mark depended on Matthew, why would he select only those quotations with a text-form relatively close to the standard versions of the Septuagint? Matthew, on the other hand, might be expected to go his own way in rendering Old Testament passages when he was not relying on Mark.[14]

Fourth, the minor agreements of Matthew and Luke against Mark, long held to be a problem for Markan priority and the Q hypothesis, continue to be heavily studied. A symposium in Göttingen and a study by Andreas Ennulat have identified, categorized, and tried to explain these agreements in massive detail,[15] but perhaps the most helpful recent study is a short article by Robert Stein. After listing eight of the most common explanations of these minor agreements, Stein points out that a parallel phenomenon exists when comparing John with the Synoptics. At numerous points, John agrees in wording or selection of detail with one of the Synoptics over against another, but no one argues on this basis that John is prior to the Synoptics.[16] Indeed, most find John not only later but also largely if not entirely independent from the written forms of Matthew, Mark, and Luke. It is much more likely that the overlaps noted reflect key aspects of the early Christian kerygma that at times were passed down orally in relatively fixed form.[17] The same hypothe-

14. David S. New, *Old Testament Quotations in the Synoptic Gospels, and the Two-Document Hypothesis*, SBLSCS 37 (Atlanta: Scholars, 1993).

15. Georg Strecker, ed., *Minor Agreements: Symposium Göttingen 1991*, GTA 50 (Göttingen: Vandenhoeck & Ruprecht, 1993); Andreas Ennulat, *Die "Minor Agreements": Untersuchungen zu einer offenen Frage des synoptischen Problems*, WUNT 2.62 (Tübingen: Mohr, 1994).

16. Robert H. Stein, "The Matthew-Luke Agreements against Mark: Insight from John," *CBQ* 54 (1992): 482–502.

17. For the most plausible conclusions of Johannine source criticism, see the introduction to my *Historicity of John* (Leicester: InterVarsity, forthcoming).

sis may well account for many of the minor agreements of Matthew and Luke against Mark.

Fifth, substantial study continues to focus on the possible overlap between Mark and Q to account for some of the minor agreements. Despite the fact that those who reject the Q hypothesis frequently complain that postulating overlapping material between these two sources is simply a convenient way to avoid problems with the two-source hypothesis, it is surely improbable that two important early accounts of portions of Jesus' life and teaching would never cover the same ground at any point. It is less clear, however, that we have any criteria that actually enable us to demonstrate the literary dependence of Mark on Q or their independence; careful studies of the question have arrived at opposing answers.[18]

Finally, proponents of virtually all positions in the debate agree that the key to establishing any other theory as superior to Markan priority is to demonstrate that the same kind of consistent and significant patterns of redaction—both stylistic and theological—that the two-source hypothesis has spawned emerge when one assumes that Mark is not first.[19] The only full-scale commentary on Mark that has attempted to do this, by C. S. Mann in the Anchor Bible series, contains precious few actual exegetical observations to this end, after a voluminous introduction,[20] while Sherman Johnson has produced a monograph comparing Markan priority and posteriority and showing how numerous key themes in the Synoptics would appear with each.[21] Judicious in his conclusions and recognizing that the data do not unilaterally support any one theory, Johnson nevertheless determines that, overall, Markan priority makes best sense of the data.

18. Supporting independence is Joachim Schüling, *Studien zum Verhältnis von Logienquelle und Markusevangelium*, FB 65 (Würzburg: Echter, 1991). Supporting dependence is Harry T. Fleddermann, *Mark and Q: A Study of the Overlap Texts*, BETL 122 (Leuven: Leuven University Press, 1995).

19. This was one of the few points of formal agreement among the large number of participants in a 1984 conference in Jerusalem, published as David L. Dungan, ed., *The Interrelations of the Gospels*, BETL 95 (Leuven: Leuven University Press, 1990); see p. 609.

20. C. S. Mann, *Mark*, AB 27 (Garden City, N.Y.: Doubleday, 1986).

21. Sherman E. Johnson, *The Griesbach Hypothesis and Redaction Criticism*, SBLMS 41 (Atlanta: Scholars, 1991).

The Q Hypothesis

If Markan priority has generated a relatively small amount of scholarly study in the last decade or so, the same can scarcely be said of the Q hypothesis. Initially, this theory was relatively modest and noncontroversial. A source of primarily sayings material was postulated to account for material that Matthew and Luke have in common not found in Mark, once it was determined that neither Matthew nor Luke uniformly demonstrates the tendencies that would be needed to claim direct literary dependence of one upon the other.[22] More recently, however, enormous amounts of literature have churned from the presses analyzing the contents, structure, theology, tradition-history, rhetoric, sociology, and audience of this hypothetical source.[23] The International Q Project is the name given to the work of a group organized by the Society of Biblical Literature to publish a series of detailed volumes on every pericope supposed to have been in Q, complete with a thorough history of scholarly opinion on virtually every word and phrase in the text, culminating in a reconstruction of the most likely original Greek form of the passage.[24]

Among the plethora of studies by those who believe that Q existed, we may discern four broad categories. First, and probably best known, is a small and very radical group of scholars, made famous in North America by their disproportionately large representation in the Jesus Seminar. These would argue that the earliest form of Q portrays Jesus as an itinerant teacher and sage, closely parallel to the countercultural Cynics of the Greco-Roman world of his day. Within this category, pride of place goes to Burton Mack and John Dominic Crossan for their

22. Scholars debate who originated the concept, but a good case can be made for Friedrich Schleiermacher in the early 1800s, who, while more famous for his recontextualizing the gospel in various "liberal" directions to try to appeal to the "cultured despisers of religion" of his day, actually retained relatively conservative opinions about the Gospels' trustworthiness.

23. See, for example, F. Neirynck, J. Verheyden, and R. Corstjens, *The Gospel of Matthew and the Sayings Source Q: A Cumulative Bibliography 1950–1995*, 2 vols., BETL 140 (Leuven: Leuven University Press, 1998).

24. For a description of the project, see James M. Robinson, "A Critical Text of the Sayings Gospel Q," *RHPR* 72 (1992): 15–22. Volumes have been appearing since 1996 under the title *Documenta Q* (Leuven: Peeters).

lengthy unpacking of this hypothesis.[25] Less well-known but also less overstated are the works of the British scholar F. G. Downing, who would otherwise significantly distance himself from the conclusions of the Jesus Seminar.[26] Important refutations of this position appear in an article by Christopher Tuckett and a book by Gregory Boyd.[27] Most important, perhaps, are the observations that of all the Greco-Roman philosophies Cynicism seems to have made the least inroads into Israel and that the very texts that most call to mind Cynic behavior (Mark 6:7–13 pars.) find Jesus commanding the disciples to forgo the characteristic beggar's purse of the Cynic itinerant.

The second category of Q studies comes closest to forming a current consensus. While not explicitly arguing that Jesus resembled a Cynic philosopher, a significant number of scholars, particularly in North America, have concluded that the earliest strata of Q portray Jesus as a merely human sage, dispensing wisdom with notable parallels to Deuteronomy, playing down the apocalyptic elements that later tradition would add back in, and outlining an ethical manifesto of compassion for the social underdog and love for one's enemies that remains a timely challenge for people today in a world filled with racism, sexism, and tribalism. John Kloppenborg from Toronto is often credited with best articulating this perspective, with whom one might compare especially Arland Jacobson and James Robinson.[28]

The third group, particularly prominent in Britain, carries on the consensus tradition of a previous generation and inverts the

25. See esp. Burton L. Mack, *The Lost Gospel: The Book of Q and Christian Origins* (San Francisco: HarperSanFrancisco, 1993); John Dominic Crossan, *The Historical Jesus: The Life of a Mediterranean Jewish Peasant* (San Francisco: HarperSanFrancisco, 1991).

26. See esp. F. Gerald Downing, *Christ and the Cynics*, JSOTMan 4 (Sheffield: JSOT, 1988). See also Leif E. Vaage, *Galilean Upstarts: Jesus' First Followers according to Q* (Valley Forge, Pa.: Trinity, 1994).

27. Christopher M. Tuckett, "A Cynic Q?" *Bib* 69 (1988): 196–225; Gregory A. Boyd, *Cynic, Sage or Son of God?* (Wheaton, Ill.: Victor, 1995).

28. See esp. John S. Kloppenborg, *The Formation of Q: Trajectories in Ancient Wisdom Collections* (Philadelphia: Fortress, 1987); idem, ed., *Conflict and Invention: Literary, Rhetorical, and Social Studies on the Sayings Gospel Q* (Valley Forge, Pa.: Trinity, 1995); Arland D. Jacobson, *The First Gospel: An Introduction to Q* (Sonoma: Polebridge, 1992); James M. Robinson, "The Real Jesus of the Sayings Gospel Q," *PSB* 18 (1997): 135–51.

tradition-history of the recent North American trend. According to this position, the earliest layers of Q contain sufficient apocalyptic material for us to label Jesus a prophet operating within very Jewish categories and calling people to repentance in light of the coming end of the world. The more sapiential material often reflects the later stages of tradition (but this position stresses, too, that prophecy and wisdom are regularly mixed together by single authors in ancient Jewish literature), and the results for historical Jesus research leave the oldest material portraying a figure less distinct from the composite picture of the final form of the Synoptics than with either of the two preceding positions. Here one thinks especially of a trio of British scholars, Christopher Tuckett, David Catchpole, and Ronald Piper.[29] Among North American studies one should highlight the writings of Dale Allison and, among recent German works, the dissertation of Migaku Sato.[30]

A fourth perspective, while relatively new and presently poorly represented, actually holds out the most promise of all. In an age when biblical scholars are consistently focusing on the final or canonical forms of texts, it is a bit anachronistic to see so much hypothetical tradition-history emanating from Q studies. Evangelical scholar Edward Meadors, in his Aberdeen University doctoral thesis, takes the Q material as it stands in Matthew and Luke, compares it with Mark, and argues that the Christologies that emerge are fully compatible with each other, reflect a high view of Jesus from the earliest stages of the tradition onward, and can be used to buttress a conservative portrait of the historical Jesus.[31] Less explicitly apologetic in its function

---

29. Christopher M. Tuckett, *Q and the History of Early Christianity: Studies on Q* (Edinburgh: T. & T. Clark; Peabody, Mass.: Hendrickson, 1996); David R. Catchpole, *The Quest for Q* (Edinburgh: T. & T. Clark, 1993); Ronald A. Piper, *Wisdom in the Q Tradition: The Aphoristic Teaching of Jesus*, SNTSMS 61 (Cambridge: Cambridge University Press, 1989).

30. See esp. Dale C. Allison, *The Jesus Tradition in Q* (Harrisburg, Pa.: Trinity, 1997); Migaku Sato, *Q und Prophetie*, WUNT 2.29 (Tübingen: Mohr, 1988). Representing the older consensus, see esp. Siegfried Schulz, *Q: Die Spruchquelle der Evangelisten* (Zürich: Theologischer, 1972); Paul Hoffmann, *Studien zur Theologie der Logienquelle*, NTAbh 8 (Münster: Aschendorff, 1972).

31. Edward P. Meadors, *Jesus the Messianic Herald of Salvation*, WUNT 2.72 (Tübingen: Mohr, 1995). Cf. idem, "The 'Messianic' Implications of the Q Material," *JBL* 118 (1999): 253–77.

is the University of Toronto dissertation of Alan Kirk. Kirk nevertheless argues even more powerfully for an analysis of the "final form" of Q, focusing especially on its genre as a collection of wisdom sayings with a coherent structure and rhetorical form that eliminate the need for parceling it out into hypothetical layers of tradition.[32]

In addition to these various perspectives that all agree that Q eventually became a coherent document, if it was not one originally, one may still find numerous authors speculating about different recensions for Q, separate documents that together form what scholars have wrongly united under the label Q, oral traditions rather than written sources, and a variety of combinations of any or all of these hypotheses.[33]

It is astonishing to observe the confidence with which various scholars compound speculative hypotheses to create elaborate reconstructions of the history of the formation of Q, the nature of the supposed itinerant preachers who created it, and the makeup of the Q community to which this document was addressed. Not that every single theory is implausible in itself, but taken together, their probability markedly diminishes; for example, three suppositions each of which may have a 60 percent

32. Alan Kirk, *The Composition of the Sayings Source: Genre, Synchrony, and Wisdom Redaction in Q*, NovTSup 91 (Leiden: Brill, 1998). Cf. idem, "Crossing the Boundary: Liminality and Transformative Wisdom in Q," *NTS* 45 (1999): 1–18.

33. For example, I. Howard Marshall (*The Gospel of Luke*, NIGTC 3 [Exeter: Paternoster; Grand Rapids: Eerdmans, 1978]) regularly appeals to two different recensions of Q on which Luke and Matthew depended. See also Frans Neirynck, "QMt and QLk and the Reconstruction of Q," *ETL* 66 (1990): 385–90. Hans Dieter Betz (*The Sermon on the Mount* [Minneapolis: Fortress, 1995]) is well known for his views that separate sources underlay Matthew's Sermon on the Mount and Luke's Sermon on the Plain, unrelated to conventional understandings of Q. Paul Hoffmann critiques this approach in his "Betz and Q," *ZNW* 88 (1997): 197–210. Eta Linnemann ("The Lost Gospel of Q—Fact or Fantasy?" *TJ* 17 [1996]: 3–18) thinks that all the parallels between Matthew and Luke can be accounted for by oral tradition. But she never demonstrates a plausible context in which the originally Aramaic words of Jesus, initially transmitted in that language by Jesus' Jewish apostles, would have been translated into Greek as part of oral tradition in a fixed enough form to create the amount of verbal parallelism that now exists. In defense of Q as written rather than oral, and in a form more or less the same for both Matthew and Luke, see now Charles E. Carlston and Dennis Norlin, "Statistics and Q—Some Further Observations," *NovT* 41 (1999): 108–23.

chance of being true (i.e., more likely than not) have only a 21.6 percent probability of all being true simultaneously. That we have the criteria to discern separate stages in the formation of Q, even if they existed, is doubtful; witness the diametrically opposite results of the "consensuses" of successive generations of scholarship that have tried this. But the more the Q material makes sense as a whole, the less need we have even to postulate such stages at all.

Richard Bauckham's important recent work, *The Gospels for All Christians*, collecting together studies related to the intentions of the evangelists in the dissemination of the Gospels, suggests that we have significantly overestimated how adequately we can reconstruct distinctive communities to which Matthew, Mark, and Luke were addressed, and that the Gospels were all initially targeted for a much wider audience than one solitary Christian church.[34] Even if the thesis of this anthology is somewhat overstated, it remains generally persuasive.[35] How much less, then, can we claim to discern in detail the nature of any hypothetical Q community! And a question too infrequently asked is, "When is an apparent parallel a genuine parallel?" Many of the sayings ascribed to Q appear in different settings in Matthew and Luke. Every good itinerant teacher repeats teachings on multiple occasions, so we must allow for this variety in the teaching of Jesus as well to account for at least some of the so-called parallels.[36]

On the other hand, I am not convinced by those who dispense with Q altogether. The Coptic *Gospel of Thomas* demonstrates that collections of largely sayings material attributed to Jesus were widely known in the early church. The genre of wisdom teachings of wise sages had become standard in the ancient world—from the teachings of the Egyptian Amen-emope to the biblical Proverbs, to the intertestamental wisdom of Sirach, to

34. Subtitled *Rethinking the Gospel Audiences* (Grand Rapids and Cambridge: Eerdmans, 1998).

35. I have indicated in my introductions to each of the four Gospels in *Jesus and the Gospels* (pp. 121–23, 133–35, 150–52, 167–70) a bare minimum of what I think can be discerned about each of these communities, and I see nothing in Bauckham's work that overturns these conclusions.

36. I have explored this issue further in "When Is a Parallel Really a Parallel? A Test Case: The Lucan Parables," *WTJ* 46 (1984): 78–103.

Greco-Roman collections of chriae or aphorisms of philoso-
phers. It would be surprising if early Christians never created
such a compendium of "the best of Jesus." That we have never
recovered such a document does not weigh against the hypothesis very forcefully. The Old Testament cites a dozen or more lost
sources for its historical material, Greco-Roman historians and
biographers regularly relied on similar written sources that no
longer exist, and, after all, it is not quite right to say that Q no
longer exists, since on the Q hypothesis, it *does* exist—embedded in both Matthew and Luke. If indeed one or both of these
Gospels reproduced most or all of Q, then it is not surprising
that there would have been little felt need to preserve a document that Christians believed was not inspired in the same way
the canonical Gospels were. And it is certainly inappropriate for
evangelicals to censor their peers who postulate the existence of
Q in this cautious way, as happened to me when I wrote an article for the *Criswell Theological Review* in the late 1980s and was
not allowed to support, however tentatively, the idea of Q by using it as a symbol for the "double tradition," but had to substitute instead "the teachings common to Matthew and Luke" at
each point into my manuscript![37]

L and M

Less secure than Markan priority and the Q hypothesis are
theories of additional written sources for Luke's and Matthew's
distinctive material. L is more probable than M simply because
Luke was not an eyewitness of the events he recorded, whereas
if Matthew was written by the apostle by that name, M might
well stand for his "memory"! In the English-speaking world, the
only recent book-length study of L is by Kim Paffenroth, who
isolates a variety of linguistic and formal features that he believes can help distinguish a Lukan source from Lukan redaction. He reconstructs a reasonably coherent narrative of 164
verses that begin and end with Jesus preaching to the outcasts:
to tax collectors, widows, and lepers, in that order, at the outset
(Luke 3:10–14; 4:25–27), and to lepers, widows, and tax collectors (the reverse order) at the end (17:12–18; 18:2–8a, 10–14a;

---

37. Craig L. Blomberg, "Elijah, Election, and the Use of Malachi in the New
Testament," *CTR* 2 (1987): 99–117.

19:2–10).[38] In German, the commentary by Gerd Petzke on peculiarly Lukan material presupposes the L hypothesis but does not further advance the case for it.[39] Bertram Pittner attempts to isolate linguistic, grammatical, and theological distinctives of L,[40] but the results remarkably resemble lists of items often attributed to Lukan redactional preference. More persuasive are studies of shorter segments of uniquely Lukan texts. Stephen Farris's case for a separate, Hebraic source for Luke's infancy narratives (chs. 1–2)[41] still stands without refutation, while several authors have found something of merit in my proposal that a chiastically arranged parable source underlies Luke's central section (9:51–18:14).[42]

The last book-length study on M in English is Stephenson Brooks's attempt to reconstruct an M community.[43] In German, again two volumes stand out but largely cancel each other out: Hans-Theo Wrege's commentary presupposing M and Hans Klein's demonstration that so-called M material and Matthean redaction substantially overlap.[44] On the other hand, it is interesting that the early church fathers regularly quote or allude to teachings of Jesus found in Matthew more than those found in any other Gospel and that a disproportionately large number of these references come from uniquely Matthean material. It is arguable, therefore, that they knew of a separate collection of sayings, either oral or written, distinct

38. Kim Paffenroth, *The Story of Jesus according to L*, JSNTSup 147 (Sheffield: Sheffield Academic, 1997).

39. Gerd Petzke, *Das Sondergut des Evangeliums nach Lukas*, ZWB (Zürich: Theologischer, 1990).

40. Bertram Pittner, *Studien zum lukanischen Sondergut*, ETS 18 (Leipzig: Benno, 1991).

41. Stephen C. Farris, *The Hymns of Luke's Infancy Narratives*, JSNTSup 9 (Sheffield: JSOT, 1985).

42. Craig L. Blomberg, "Midrash, Chiasmus, and the Outline of Luke's Central Section," in *Studies in Midrash and Historiography*, vol. 3 of *Gospel Perspectives*, ed. R. T. France and David Wenham (Sheffield: JSOT, 1983), 217–61. Cf. esp. John Nolland, *Luke*, vol. 2, WBC 35B (Dallas: Word, 1993), 530–31; Bock, *Luke*, 2:961–64.

43. Stephenson H. Brooks, *Matthew's Special Community: The Evidence of His Special Sayings Material*, JSNTSup 16 (Sheffield: JSOT, 1987).

44. Hans-Theo Wrege, *Das Sondergut des Matthäus-Evangeliums*, ZWB (Zürich: Theologischer, 1991); Hans Klein, *Bewährung im Glauben: Studien zum Sondergut des Evangelisten Matthäus* (Neukirchen-Vluyn: Neukirchener, 1996).

from canonical Matthew, that was also one of Matthew's sources.[45]

The Griesbach Hypothesis and Lukan Use of Matthew

The major challenge to the two- (or four-) source hypothesis over the last forty years has been what is increasingly called the two-Gospel hypothesis. Following the lead of the late-eighteenth-century German scholar, Johann Jakob Griesbach, this view stands Markan priority on its head and argues that Mark was the last of the Synoptics to be written. Much like various Greco-Roman historians who substantially abbreviated their sources, Mark is believed to have abridged and conflated both Matthew and Luke. Luke's Gospel itself was derived directly from Matthew's, which thus turns out to be the earliest Gospel, in keeping with consistent patristic testimony.[46]

No one has worked more tirelessly to champion this perspective than William Farmer, particularly through a long series of international conferences.[47] Farmer's most recent book-length work focuses particularly on the pastoral relevance of the Synoptic problem. There he observes that advocates of Markan priority and the Q hypothesis regularly conclude that only a small portion of the Synoptics is historical and the Jesus they reconstruct greatly differs from orthodox portraits. He recognizes that this is not true for conservative scholars who accept the two-source hypothesis but argues that this is because they do not really carry through their source-critical presuppositions to their logical conclusions. Thus, the Griesbach hypothesis, with a Mark who abridges rather than a Matthew and Luke who embellish, is more amenable to conservative theology.[48]

45. See Craig L. Blomberg, *The Historical Reliability of the Gospels* (Leicester and Downers Grove, Ill.: InterVarsity, 1987), 206–8, and the literature there cited.

46. For this testimony, see the introductory sections to any of the standard commentaries on Matthew; for example, Craig L. Blomberg, *Matthew* (Nashville: Broadman, 1992), 34–46.

47. For a complete list of these, see Dungan, *History*, 377–78.

48. William R. Farmer, *The Gospel of Jesus: The Pastoral Relevance of the Synoptic Problem* (Louisville: Westminster John Knox, 1994).

As should be clear by now, I disagree that the two-source hypothesis requires these radical appendages. Only if one does not allow for Matthew and Luke to have had access to reliable information for their nonparalleled material is one forced to reject historicity. And while many two-source supporters make this claim, it has nothing to do with assumptions about Markan priority and Q per se. Second, I would stress that conservatives dare not gravitate toward a particular hypothesis simply because it is apologetically convenient; we must follow where the data lead regardless of the results. Evangelical Christians have too frequently taken the easy route and opted for something that is less than fully intellectually honest;[49] we must not deliberately perpetuate the trend! Third, Griesbach himself was no friend of orthodoxy, and there is a broad conservative-to-liberal spectrum among advocates of his approach, as there is with supporters of the two-source hypothesis. Finally, as I mentioned above, the major weakness in the Griesbach theory to date is that its proponents have not demonstrated how Markan style and theology emerge more consistently and coherently on their hypothesis than on the alternatives. Until I see such a demonstration, I will remain unconvinced.

On the other hand, attempts have been made to trace in detail Luke's direct use of Matthew. Two particular studies stand out above all others here. On the one hand, Michael Goulder in England has penned a massive two-volume introduction and source-critical commentary on Luke arguing, with Markan priorists, that Luke did depend on Mark but, against the Q hypothesis, that Luke directly depended on Matthew. Everything else in Luke's Gospel is his own redaction, which for Goulder almost always means creation, apart from any other sources.[50] The volumes reflect a prodigious tour de force, but they are not written with a comparative format, arguing for the greater plausibility of Luke's use of Matthew than of his use of Q and/or L. Instead, they almost always present speculation as to what Luke might

49. See esp. Mark A. Noll, *The Scandal of the Evangelical Mind* (Grand Rapids: Eerdmans; Leicester: InterVarsity, 1994).

50. Michael D. Goulder, *Luke: A New Paradigm*, 2 vols., JSNTSup 20 (Sheffield: JSOT, 1989). For a curious attempt further to defend "fatigue" as a convincing explanation for Lukan redaction, see Mark Goodacre, "Fatigue in the Synoptics," *NTS* 44 (1998): 45–58.

have done *if* he directly depended on Matthew and Mark but no one else. And the speculations consistently defy credibility: Luke jumps all over the place in drawing on his sources, is inconsistent in his redactional practices because he grows weary, omits entire passages becauses he knows he will later substitute a small portion of them in entirely different contexts (or has already done so), and so on. F. G. Downing has subjected Goulder's hypothesis to intense scrutiny, stressing among other things that the sheer mechanics of copying from scrolls in antiquity weigh strongly against any author jumping around in the use of sources in such a hodge-podge fashion.[51] Sharon Mattila builds on Downing's work to demonstrate that the classical historians who provide partial parallels to the hypothesis of Mark and/or Luke abridging their sources also consistently and thoroughly rewrote their sources in ways that make the originals far more difficult to reconstruct than on *any* of the standard theories of Gospel origins.[52]

Only slightly more plausible is the second major study attempting to demonstrate coherent Lukan redaction of Matthew, this one by advocates of the Griesbach hypothesis: McNicol, Dungan, and Peabody. Like Goulder, they do not attempt to show how Luke's use of Matthew is more probable than his use of Mark and Q, but merely what his redactional approach could have been on the assumption of his use of Matthew. One of the findings they laud as much as any is their observation that Luke's parallels with Matthew in Luke 3:1–10:22 can be accounted for by the assumption that Luke proceeded through Matthew 3:1–18:5 five times, borrowing and modifying material in Matthew's sequence each time.[53] But statistically this is not that significant: if one postulates a writer retracing his or her steps consecutively through a supposed source often enough, any two sequences of material can be made to line up with each other! And the majority of Luke's double-tradition material comes in the rest of his Gospel,

51. F. Gerald Downing, "A Paradigm Perplex: Luke, Matthew and Mark," *NTS* 38 (1992): 15–36.

52. Sharon L. Mattila, "A Question Too Often Neglected," *NTS* 41 (1995): 199–217. For an important and more sympathetic book-length critique of Goulder, see Mark S. Goodacre, *Goulder and the Gospels: An Examination of a New Paradigm*, JSNTSup 133 (Sheffield: Sheffield Academic, 1996).

53. McNicol with Dungan and Peabody, *Beyond the Q Impasse*.

where all the authors of this study can say is that Luke has mined Matthew "often" taking him in sequence.[54] Interestingly, this is exactly the reverse of what Goulder claims is one of the most overlooked strengths of his work, that Luke has proceeded through Matthew in *reverse* order for nine consecutive stages of Luke 12:22–18:8.[55] Neither proposed procedure is convincing; together, they largely cancel each other out.[56]

Other Theories of Matthean Priority

No one, to my knowledge, has recently come out with any detailed development of the approach traditionally[57] ascribed to Augustine: Matthew comes first, Mark depends on Matthew, and Luke uses both Matthew and Mark. But there are those who recognize that the internal as well as the external evidence make the relationship between Matthew and Mark more complex than the relatively straightforward dependence of Luke on Mark. To take just one example, there are so many Semitisms and other signs of primitive tradition in Matthew's distinctive "additions" to the dialogue between Peter and Jesus on the road to Caesarea Philippi (Matt. 16:13–20) that even scholars who otherwise support Markan priority argue for authenticity and even Matthean priority here.[58] Clearly, the strongest argument

54. Ibid., chart C, detachable foldout in back pocket.

55. Goulder, *Luke*, 2:582. For his complaint, see Michael D. Goulder, "Is Q a Juggernaut?" *JBL* 115 (1996): 667–81. He moderates his criticism of the Q hypothesis somewhat in "Self-Contradiction in the IQP," *JBL* 118 (1999): 506–17. For further critique of McNicol with Dungan and Peabody, see Mark Goodacre, "*Beyond the Q Impasse* or Down a Blind Alley?" *JSNT* 76 (1999): 33–52.

56. Another important study, highly touted by Griesbachians, but in fact aligning itself with no one solution to the Synoptic problem is David J. Neville, *Arguments from Order in Synoptic Source Criticism: A History and Critique*, NGS 7 (Leuven: Peeters, 1993; Macon, Ga.: Mercer University Press, 1994). What Neville does show is that the various arguments from the order of Matthew's and Luke's Markan parallels do not consistently support Markan priority.

57. I say "traditionally" because advocates of the Griesbach hypothesis sometimes argue that a passage from later in Augustine's writings (*Harmony of the Gospels* 4.10.11) can be taken as support for his changing his mind and favoring the order Matthew, Luke, Mark, but this is not the most natural reading of Augustine's text.

58. See esp. Ben F. Meyer, *The Aims of Jesus* (London: SCM, 1979), 185–97.

in favor of Matthean priority is the consistent patristic testimony, from Papias onward.

A perspective that surfaces from time to time in various
strands of scholarship deserves, in my opinion, more detailed
investigation, namely, the possibility that the *logia* to which Papias referred were in fact something like what scholars today
call Q.[59] The argument that in Papias's earlier testimony about
Mark he uses *logia* to refer to the entire Gospel does not seem
cogent: Papias's entire phrase is "an ordered collection of the
Lord's *logia*," an expression in which the word *collection* refers
to the whole and *logia* to its constituent elements. Thus, when
Papias continues by referring to Matthew composing his *logia*
in the Hebrew language and everyone translating as they were
able (Eusebius, *Hist. eccl.* 3.39.14–16), the natural interpretation
is to understand *logia* as less than the entire Gospel we now call
Matthew. That this completed Gospel depended on Mark as well
as on what we might call proto-Matthew, itself conceivably
translated into Greek at some stage, does not seem to me at all
implausible. Perhaps, then, this is the one place where my sequence of theories corresponds only to frequency of advocacy
and not also to probability. When David Black and I were nego-
tiating my role in this symposium, I proposed doing a shorter
paper on the specific hypothesis of proto-Matthew instead of
this longer overview of positions, but I lost!

More-Complex Hypotheses

Once much more popular than they are now, from time to
time theories again surface that postulate one or more original
Gospel narratives larger than any (or even all) of our canonical
texts. These have often been proposed to avoid theories of more
direct literary dependence of one Synoptic on another and have
generally failed to convince.[60] But more modest hypotheses,

59. See, for example, T. W. Manson, *The Sayings of Jesus* (London: SCM,
1949), 16–20; Matthew Black, "The Use of Rhetorical Terminology in Papias on
Mark and Matthew," *JSNT* 37 (1989): 31–41; Donald A. Hagner, *Matthew*, vol. 1,
WBC 33A (Dallas: Word, 1994), xlvi.
60. But see J. C. O'Neill, "The Lost Written Records of Jesus' Words and
Deeds Behind Our Records," *JTS* 42 (1991): 483–503.

such as longer records of individual sermons of Jesus being abbreviated by the various evangelists, merit further analysis. David Wenham's entire book on how this might work for the Olivet discourse has scarcely been refuted;[61] it has largely been ignored. On a much smaller scale, George Kennedy's suggestion that the Sermons on the Mount and Plain might be treated similarly deserves thorough unpacking.[62]

One explanation of some of the minor agreements of Matthew and Luke against Mark, of course, has always been to postulate a proto-Mark on which canonical Matthew, Mark, and Luke all depended. Evidence like that for a proto-Matthew discussed above has suggested to M.-É Boismard a solution to the Synoptic problem that finds all three Synoptics depending on both proto-Matthew and proto-Mark.[63] In his earlier writings, Boismard had proposed an even more complicated hypothesis in which every Gospel, as we know them, used a prior version of at least two of the other Gospels.[64] E. P. Sanders and Margaret Davies present in accessible form these and other hypotheses still more complex, several of which are otherwise associated only with French-language studies.[65] They conclude that it is inherently probable that a comprehensive solution to the Synoptic problem is not to be found by applying Occam's razor (the simpler the hypothesis, the better), and that we probably will never be able to trace a complete solution.[66] I tend to agree, not least because writers of ancient history and biography were routinely influenced by a multiplicity of oral and written sources at numerous stages in the composition of their works. But I am not prepared to give up the exercise of ranking respective probabilities of various solutions, and it

61. David Wenham, *The Rediscovery of Jesus' Eschatological Discourse*, vol. 4 of *Gospel Perspectives* (Sheffield: JSOT, 1984).

62. George A. Kennedy, *New Testament Interpretation through Rhetorical Criticism* (Chapel Hill: University of North Carolina Press, 1984), 67–69.

63. See, for example, his entire section entitled "The Multiple-Stage Hypothesis," in Dungan, ed., *Interrelations of the Gospels*, 231–88.

64. P. Benoit and M.-É Boismard, *Synopse des quatre évangiles*, vol. 2 (Paris: Cerf, 1972), 17.

65. E. P. Sanders and Margaret Davies, *Studying the Synoptic Gospels* (London: SCM; Philadelphia: Trinity, 1989), 93–111. Cf. now also Philippe Rolland, "A New Look at the Synoptic Question," *EuroJTh* 8 (1999): 133–44.

66. Sanders and Davies, *Studying*, 112–19.

still appears that the two- (or four-) source hypothesis, possibly modified to allow for a proto-Matthew, which just might resemble what we call Q, stands a better chance of being on target than any of the alternatives.

Other Theories

Other suggestions must be treated rapidly. Robert Lindsey (recently deceased), longtime Baptist missionary in Israel, convinced a handful of scholars based in Jerusalem that Luke should be seen as the first Synoptic Gospel, on which the others depended, largely because he thought that it translated most easily back into Hebrew.[67] Few others who have replicated the experiment agree. I mention the theory here only because many American evangelicals will encounter its supporters if they visit, even for short-term study tours, as many do, the Jerusalem University College, formerly known as the American Institute of Holy Land Studies on Mt. Zion.

More recently, Ronald Huggins has championed what he calls Matthean posteriority. But his study does not so much advance evidence for treating Matthew as later than both Mark and Luke as observe that a better case can be made for Matthew using Luke than Luke using Matthew for the double-tradition material.[68] This causes problems for Goulder and the Griesbachians but not for proponents of Q, since they have regularly observed that Luke seems to modify Q less than Matthew does.

Still others from time to time suggest that part or all of that which is normally ascribed to literary dependence can be accounted for by oral traditions preserved in a relatively fixed form. Twenty years ago, classical historian John Rist argued this for Matthew and Mark (but not for Luke and Mark), after observing how part of the time Matthew seems older and part of the time Mark does.[69] But our suggestions about proto-Mat-

---

67. See Robert L. Lindsey, "A Modified Two-Document Theory of the Synoptic Dependence and Interdependence," *NovT* 6 (1963): 239–63.

68. Ronald V. Huggins, "Matthean Posteriority: A Preliminary Proposal," *NovT* 34 (1992): 1–22.

69. John Rist, *On the Independence of Matthew and Mark*, SNTSMS 32 (Cambridge: Cambridge University Press, 1979).

thew can account for these data as well. Scholars such as Albert Lord and Bruce Chilton have argued for a substantial influence of oral tradition, based on models from comparative folklore and rabbinic materials, respectively.[70] Bo Reicke overlooked the fundamental meaning of "narrative" in Luke's prologue as a "written source" to argue that only oral traditions are there referenced.[71] And Eta Linnemann vents her displeasure with the radical higher critics' stranglehold on scholarship, particularly in Germany, by minimizing the verbal parallelism among the Synoptics and arguing exclusively for dependence on reliable, oral tradition. But even her relatively smaller percentages (46.5 percent parallelism between Matthew and Mark; 36.2 percent between Luke and Mark)[72] are greater than what we often find in various writers like Josephus, even when they are rewriting their own previously written documents to create new works![73]

The late British evangelical John Wenham, who for years argued for earlier dates for the Synoptics than just about any other scholar, and who was very sympathetic to oral tradition influencing all of the Gospels all the way through the final stages of composition, nevertheless recognized that literary dependence cannot be dispensed with altogether for three fundamental reasons: (1) the frequent agreement in order of pericopae when there is no chronological necessity for preserving that order; (2) the quick and widespread dissemination of the Gospels in the early church; and (3) the improbability of all four evangelists inventing the identical genre independently of each other for their accounts of the life of

70. Albert B. Lord, "The Gospels as Oral Traditional Literature," in *The Relationships among the Gospels*, ed. William O. Walker Jr., TUMSR 5 (San Antonio: Trinity University Press, 1978), 33–91; Bruce D. Chilton, *Profiles of a Rabbi: Synoptic Opportunities in Reading about Jesus*, BJS 177 (Atlanta: Scholars, 1989).

71. Bo Reicke, *The Roots of the Synoptic Gospels* (Philadelphia: Fortress, 1986), 45.

72. Eta Linnemann, *Is There a Synoptic Problem? Rethinking the Literary Dependence of the First Three Gospels* (Grand Rapids: Baker, 1992), 108.

73. See F. G. Downing, "Redaction Criticism: Josephus' *Antiquities* and the Synoptic Gospels," *JSNT* 8 (1980): 46–65; 9 (1980): 29–48. And Downing is quite sympathetic to the influence of oral tradition on the Synoptics; witness his "Word Processing in the Ancient World: The Social Production and Performance of Q," *JSNT* 64 (1996): 29–48.

Christ.[74] I would add that no theories of literary independence have ever explained why one Gospel should mimic another with respect to narrative asides, such as those found in
Mark 2:10–11 pars. ("But that you may know that the Son of
man has authority on earth to forgive sins"—he said to the
paralytic—"I say to you. . . .") and elsewhere.

Final Remarks

I have already expressed my preference for a modified two-
(or four-) source hypothesis that allows for some form of proto-
Matthew. But my mandate here has been primarily to outline
the options. I cannot conclude, however, without making some
reference to a work that would have you believe that those of us
who believe in some kind of literary dependence among the
Synoptics are thereby unwittingly disabled by "satanic blind-
ness." I speak, of course, of *The Jesus Crisis*, edited and contrib-
uted to by Robert L. Thomas and F. David Farnell.[75] It is a book
that made me alternately sad and angry as I read it, in that it is
rife with inappropriately sharp polemic against virtually all
evangelical Gospel scholars, regularly misrepresents them, contains numerous typographical and factual errors, and offers no
detailed inductive or exegetical study of Gospel parallels that
would support the alternative of literary independence, which
the editors view as the only position consistent with inerrancy.[76]
I was all the more perplexed when I discovered in *Faith and Mission*, the academic journal of the institution sponsoring the
symposium that generated the present volume, a remarkably
positive review of Thomas and Farnell's book, which even per-

74. John Wenham, *Redating Matthew, Mark and Luke: A Fresh Assault on the
Synoptic Problem* (London: Hodder & Stoughton, 1991; Downers Grove, Ill.:
InterVarsity, 1992), 9–10.

75. Subtitled *The Inroads of Historical Criticism into Evangelical Scholarship*
(Grand Rapids: Kregel, 1998). The quotation comes from Thomas's epilogue,
p. 380.

76. For a small sampling of these errors and misrepresentations, one may
compare the references to and quotations of my work on pp. 22, 31, 32, 34, 83,
324, 346, 347, 348, 354, 364, 368, 372, 373, and 385 with the original contents
and contexts of my writings.

petuated (hopefully, unwittingly) one of Thomas's numerous misrepresentations of my own work.[77]

Thomas and Farnell do, however, occasionally make significant points. One of them is that the Synoptic problem is an important matter. I did not always think so as a student; my students do not always think so now. When it is treated in isolation from the other components of the formation of the Gospels, this reaction is at least in part understandable. When we recognize the solution to the Synoptic problem to be a central building block in our understanding of how to answer questions about the trustworthiness of the Gospels and the distinctive theologies of each evangelist, we cannot help but appreciate its importance. So let the discussions proceed, but let them proceed in an irenic and not a polemic spirit, as we recognize that Scripture has not unequivocally revealed to us the solution to the Synoptic problem.

77. L. Russ Bush, review of *The Jesus Crises* [*sic*], *Faith and Mission* 16 (1998): 120–21. On p. 121 he writes, "Blomberg's proposed theory of the New Testament's general trustworthiness is simply not good enough to establish the truthfulness of any specific event or teaching." Since Bush, as part of the editorial board of the New American Commentary, approved of my using the same approach in my *Matthew*, I can only assume that he is simply summarizing Thomas at this point, although it sounds as though he does so with approval. But then I have never claimed that inductive historical study leads to certainty, if by "establish" Bush (or Thomas) means "to be 100 percent certain." No historical method can do that, and no one argues that it does. But it is far better to be able to demonstrate "general trustworthiness," and then argue that authors should be given the benefit of the doubt where they cannot be tested when they have proved reliable where they can be tested, than to call for a faith commitment to historical reliability *despite* claiming that the majority of evidence points in the opposite direction.

2

QUESTIONS ABOUT Q

Darrell L. Bock

To be assigned an essay assessing a document that we do not have is a daunting task. One is tempted simply to say that this document does not exist, and then move on. The only question we should have about Q is why it was ever proposed to have existed at all. Obviously, Q's existence is associated with what is widely known as the two-source hypothesis and with Markan priority. Another essay by Dr. McKnight has the responsibility of treating Markan priority. However, I do feel some need to present why people believe Q existed and how they respond to those who have doubts. Thus, a discussion of the existence of Q opens our essay. In this opening section I treat how arguments against Q are made by those who do not believe the source ever existed as well as explain the rationale for arguing for the source's existence. In sum, those who hold to Matthean priority reject Q's existence largely on the basis of the external evidence of church tradition, which argued that Matthew was the first Gospel composed. In their view, there is no need to posit the existence of this hypothetical source. It is necessary to evaluate this church tradition surrounding Matthew's origin. Only then does it become clear that one should also consider issues tied to internal evidence, such as the order of units and their wording, as well as evidence for or against Luke's use of Matthew.[1] If Matthew is not the first Gospel written or there is evidence that Luke did not use Matthew, then the rationale for the existence of a source like Q becomes plausible.

A section on the character of Q follows. In particular I raise the question about the likelihood of this having been a unified documentary source or merely a "shared tradition stream" (a mix of written and oral material) that Matthew and Luke shared. This is a question that is more open and complex than current discussion suggests. In this second section I also note the nature of Q's contents. The three major themes that stand in the material receive special attention, as well as how scholars have thought about their relationship and development in Q. It is here that I also give some critical comment about what gets done in Q studies. This eventually leads into a final section where the question of how scholars have used and abused Q material receives attention. The study proceeds inductively, so conclusions come at summary or transition points.

You deserve to know that I hold to Markan priority, but that it is a position I steadily came to rather than having inherited it as an assumption in my work. My main mentor in seminary holds to Matthean priority. I remember coloring my way through a synopsis when I was in seminary, open to either of the main options held today. I was seeking answers to the source question by carefully examining the wording of the text, as well as wrestling with the testimony of the church fathers. They testified to Matthew as the earliest Gospel, or at least as the source of a main teaching

---

1. For reasons of space, I cannot go over the full debate that argues internally for Matthean priority, including the important argument made from agreements between Matthew and Luke against Mark. I will only try to make the positive case for the possibility of Q. A complete treatment would require that one deal with this argument in some detail. In fact, this essay in general focuses only on "macro" arguments of larger structures between the Gospels. The issues raised by "micro" arguments of details within are also important, but are so varied as to be difficult to pursue in a summarizing essay. For a full argument to be present, however, both macro and micro arguments need consideration.

component that went into the Gospel tradition. I have appreciated the work of those who hold to the two-Gospel theory for
keeping everyone who works in Synoptic studies honest.

As a way into the Q problem I have some things to say about
their recent work on Luke's use of Matthew, a premise that, if
true, means that I should end the paper here, for then there is
no reason to discuss the existence of Q. An examination of their
work, however, shows why Q becomes an alternative explanation of things. So I begin with questions surrounding the mere
existence of Q.

The Existence of Q

The case of the existence of Q really begins with a negative
observation. It is that Matthew and Luke do not depend on each
other. Thus, not only does belief that Q existed usually argue
that Mark is the first Gospel, but also that Luke did not use or
know Matthew.[2] This conclusion about Luke and Matthew requires that two points be treated: (1) the united testimony of the
church fathers that Matthew was the first Gospel, and (2) showing why one can believe that Luke did not use Matthew.

The issue of the church's consistent testimony that Matthew
was the first Gospel is, in my view, the strongest argument
Matthean prioritists possess.[3] This testimony comes from many
sources, though several of the sources are reported to us
through Eusebius (ca. A.D. 260–340). Some yield evidence that is
highly disputed. For example, Eusebius reports on a tradition

2. Though theoretically one could argue that Matthew used Luke, virtually
no one places Luke's writing before Matthew, so that the only option left is to
argue that Luke did not use Matthew. With regard to Markan priority, it is generally acknowledged today that the evidence of how Mark parallels the other
Synoptics makes it most likely that Mark is either the first or the last Synoptic
Gospel in the sequence. I briefly comment on Mark after considering the relationship between Matthew and Luke.

3. A second important argument for Matthean priority is the issue of
Matthean-Lukan agreements against Mark. These are often called "minor"
agreements, but that description biases the discussion. Those who hold to Markan priority argue that the number of these is not so great, given the size of the
Synoptic materials, and also argue that greater problems exist for those arguing
that Luke used Matthew or that Mark is the last Gospel. The details of this
debate extend beyond the size of this essay.

tied to Papias and his "Expositions on the Oracles of the Lord" (ca. A.D. 130–140) that "Matthew made an ordered arrangement of the oracles/gospel [τὰ λόγια] in the Hebrew [or, Aramaic] language and each one translated [or, interpreted] it as he was able" (*Hist. eccl.* 3.39.16).[4] In Eusebius, this comes after a discussion of Papias's report that Mark was the interpreter of Peter. This early testimony actually says nothing about the order of the Gospels, however. It may not even discuss the Gospel of Matthew, but simply that Matthew had a role in recording some of the Lord's teaching, although the context in which the remark appears seems more likely to be discussing the Gospel. However, even if it does mention Matthew, it does so in a Semitic form, and the Gospel we discuss in the canon is in Greek. It is debated whether Matthew as we have it was ever originally in a Semitic form. So this citation is fraught with difficulty.[5] If we accept the citation as accurate, then is it talking about the Matthew we have in the canon? If not, then can we even apply it to the debate over the order of the Synoptics? If we have reason to be uncertain about what it refers to (the Gospel or simply a record of some of Jesus' teaching), then how much can we make of its testimony?

The reason this text is viewed as important is that many argue that the subsequent church tradition stemmed from here, a point that cannot be demonstrated. For example, Irenaeus (ca.

---

4. The translation shows the points of dispute in the citation. Does *logia* refer to a collection of Jesus' teaching or to the Gospel of Matthew? Did Papias argue that the original collection was in Hebrew or in its Semitic alternative, Aramaic, which was the most widely used language among Jews of that time and thus could be called the "Hebrew dialect"? Did he allude to this collection being translated into Greek or merely interpreted? There also is the view that Papias is only referring to "Hebrew style" and not the dialect, but this seems less than clear given how this remark was accepted into the tradition as being linguistic. If the later tradition misread the remark, then we lose the problem of Papias not referring to our Matthew, but gain the problem of the tradition being wrong in how it picked up on the remark! On this last point, see Bernard Orchard and Harold Riley, *The Order of the Synoptics: Why Three Gospels?* (Macon, Ga.: Mercer University Press, 1987), 198–99, and J. Kürzinger, "Das Papiaszeugnis und die Erstgestalt des Matthäus Evangeliums," *BZ* n.f. 4 (1960): 19–38, both of whom argue that Papias is referring to Hebrew style.

5. For a nice treatment of these issues, see W. D. Davies and Dale C. Allison, *The Gospel according to Saint Matthew*, 3 vols, ICC (Edinburgh: T. & T. Clark, 1988), 1:7–17, 128–29.

A.D. 130–200) speaks of a written Gospel that Matthew published "in his own language among the Hebrews" (*apud* Eusebius, *Hist. eccl.* 5.8.2; Irenaeus, *Haer.* 3.1.1; see also Eusebius, *Hist. eccl.* 5.10.3, where mention is made of a tradition that finds Matthew in Hebrew letters in India in the mid-second century). The remark does show that Irenaeus read Papias's remark or the tradition it represents as being about the Gospel. Again our problem is that we have little evidence beyond this external testimony that Matthew, at least the version we possess in the canon, was originally in Hebrew.[6] This example shows the difficulty that can exist in the appeal to tradition. If we cannot be sure of its accuracy at one point or at several points, then what does that say about the other points the tradition makes? If we treat the citation as accurate, then is it referring to the Greek version of Matthew we use today, or simply its roots (in which case we are back into the oral tradition behind our canon but not in a discussion about the texts we possess today)?

Nonetheless, other remarks from the church fathers are more to the point of sequence. Clement of Alexandria (ca. A.D. 150–220), in a work known as *Hypotyposeis*, says, in a report coming to us through Eusebius, that he knew of a tradition from "the primitive elders" (παράδοσιν τῶν ἀνέκαθεν πρεσβυτέρων) concerning the order of the Gospels that the first written Gospels were those that contained the genealogies. Clement goes on to note that Mark summarized Peter's public preaching and John wrote last (Eusebius, *Hist. eccl.* 6.14.5–6). Origen ([ca. A.D. 185–253] *Comm. Jo.* 6:32; and *apud* Eusebius, *Hist. eccl.* 6.25.4), Eusebius (*Hist. eccl.* 3.24.5–18), and Jerome (*Vir. ill.* 3) take a similar position about the Hebrew origin and Matthean priority, but they place Mark as the second Gospel, in opposition to Clement.[7] Later, Augustine (A.D. 354–430) also defended the order Matthew-Mark-Luke, affirming the order

6. There is one reference later from Jerome, ca. A.D. 392, that he saw and copied this Gospel in its Hebrew form in Beroea in Syria (*Vir. ill.* 3).

7. This testimony is often challenged for its accuracy by Markan prioritists because it is seen as either a deduction emerging from the uncertain reference to a Hebrew original or from what had become the established sequential order for the "first" Gospels in the "fourfold" Gospel collection. Of these reasons, only the one involving the Semitic roots of Matthew may have merit as a counterargument to challenge the statement's credibility.

now in our Bibles but contradicting the remarks of Clement that the Gospels with genealogies were first, showing a lack of solidarity in the early church tradition about Gospel order (*cons.* 1.3). In this text Mark is the "footman and abbreviator" of Matthew.[8] So what the tradition does affirm consistently is that Matthew came first.

Augustine's view on Gospel sequence helped solidify Matthew-Mark-Luke as the preferred view for the church for centuries after him. But, as I noted already, this view predates him as both earlier testimony from the church fathers and from canonical lists show. Jerome (ca. A.D. 342–420) makes the same point in his prologue to the four Gospels while discussing the order of the Gospels, as does Origen as reported in Eusebius 6.25.3–6.[9] Lists suggesting what became the Augustinian sequence are the Anti-Marcionite Prologue to Luke (pre-A.D. 200) and the Muratorian Canon. This final list speaks of Luke as the third and John as the fourth Gospel (ca. A.D. 200).[10] Thus, if there is an early church view, it argues for the order of Matthew-Mark-Luke, an order that the internal evidence of the Gospels themselves seems to oppose. Again the question becomes, What part of the tradition can one regard as trustworthy? If certain portions of the tradition are unclear as to their connection to our Matthew (Papias's reference to Matthew's *logia*) or refer to an early non-Greek Matthew, then what use can be made of such points for the Matthew we use? If the issue of order is questioned today against the bulk of the tradition, then can we be confident about its statements on the specific sequence of a given Gospel?

8. This view of Augustine was recently challenged by William R. Farmer, *The Gospel of Jesus: The Pastoral Relevance of the Synoptic Problem* (Louisville: Westminster/John Knox, 1994), 17–18. He argues that Augustine may have held to the order Matthew-Luke-Mark, as the two-Gospel hypothesis argues. However, it appears that Augustine is making a literary comparison here, not a remark about sequence. Later in this same work Augustine did acknowledge that Mark had some theological development from Matthew. For an excellent collection of texts from the early church on the Gospels, see Orchard and Riley, *Order of the Synoptics,* 111–277.

9. For Jerome's text, see Orchard and Riley, *Order of the Synoptics,* 206.

10. The Gospel order for Irenaeus in *Haer.* 3.1.1 is less clear. It may be Matthew-Mark-Luke, if the order in which he discusses the Gospels is his view of their sequence. See also Eusebius, *Hist. eccl.* 5.8.1–5.

I have treated the external evidence in some detail because it is important to see its consistency and disputed elements side by side. The testimony of the early church is that Matthew is the first Gospel, but that testimony is clouded by the fact that it is a Hebrew version that is also fairly consistently alluded to in such remarks. Our uncertainty about the existence of this Hebrew version, for which there is little other evidence, makes the evidence less pristine than it might otherwise appear. Debates in the early church on other related points tied directly to Matthew's origin, like the order of the Synoptics, also raise questions about whether we can rely on the tradition on other points it makes. As I noted, this is the strongest argument for Matthean priority because of its consistency, but it is less strong than it initially appears to be because of the ambiguity in some of the arguments related to Matthew's origin.

This ambiguity in the external evidence means that consideration of internal evidence must also be undertaken. It is here that the positive case for Q's existence begins. That evidence comes in two parts: (1) that Luke did not use Matthew, and (2) that a significant portion of material shared between Luke and Matthew gives evidence of having similar roots. In preview, the argument goes like this: Can it be shown to be more likely that Luke did not use Matthew than that Luke did? If Luke did not use Matthew, then how does one explain the similarity between about 225 verses shared between Matthew and Luke, a figure that represents one-fourth of Matthew and one-fifth of Luke? When one notes that the order of this material often is parallel, then a key reason to suggest a common source emerges. It is to this argument we now turn.

In considering the question of whether Luke used Matthew, we will make two arguments. One involves the use or nonuse of key elements of Matthew at a macro structural level, while the other looks strictly at issues tied to the order of events in each of these Gospels.

The macro argument suggests that the nature of Luke shows that he did not know or use Matthew. For example, it is argued that the distinct nature of the infancy material shows no clear connection to Matthew's account. Matthew tells the story from Joseph's perspective, while Mary is the key point of reference for Luke. Now it could be claimed that Luke simply chose to supplement Matthew's account.[11] However, there are no links to Matthean details, a procedure unlike the way Luke handles parallel Passion material. Likewise, Luke's Sermon on the Plain evidences a lack of knowledge of Matthew's Sermon. Now many of the omissions in Luke's version, such as the absence of the six antitheses, could be explained as his choice not to treat issues tied to Judaism. However, what is consistently happening in Luke is that clearly organized discourses in Matthew are broken up and spread across Luke rather randomly when considered from the Matthean angle, if Luke knew and used Matthew. The question is whether such an editorial choice for Luke, though possible, is plausible, especially when the order of such scattering in Luke is so random.[12]

Just as important, from the standpoint of the Griesbach alternative, is the question of whether Mark, as the last Gospel written (according to that view), would choose to omit any evidence of this sermon entirely. The usual explanation is that Mark shuns speech material, which is true, but he does include traces of both the Olivet discourse and the kingdom parable discourse, so his tendency to omit speech material is not absolute.[13] Such

11. An important study defending and explaining Luke's supposed use of Matthew is that of Allan J. McNicol, David L. Dungan, and David B. Peabody, eds., *Beyond the Q Impasse: Luke's Use of Matthew* (Valley Forge, Pa.: Trinity, 1996). This study is the first comprehensive treatment of Lukan redaction from a Griesbachian perspective, and as such is a significant study. They claim on pp. 49–50 that Luke reflects "the essence" of Matthew's account, but substantiating this claim with any shared details is hard to see. For example, they note that both use genealogies; but Luke's genealogy is in a different locale than Matthew's and differs in significant ways from Matthew's listing. They appeal to both accounts referring to visitors and celestial signs; but the visitors are not the same and neither are the signs.

12. The following lists the order of material reappearing elsewhere in Luke that Matthew has in the sermon. The Lukan passages are cited, but the sequence of the units reflects the Matthean order: 14:34–35 (Matt. 5:13); 11:33 (Matt. 5:15); 16:17 (Matt. 5:18); 12:57–59 (Matt. 5:25–26); 16:18 (Matt. 5:31–32); 11:2–4 (Matt. 6:6–13); 12:33–34 (Matt. 6:19–21); 11:34–36 (Matt. 6:22–23); 16:13 (Matt. 6:24); 12:22–32 (Matt. 6:25–34); 11:9–13 (Matt. 7:7–11); 13:23–24 (Matt. 7:13–14); 13:25–27 (Matt. 7:22–33). One can see here how random the order of texts is.

13. The tension here of the picture of Mark is enhanced when one realizes that the claim is that Mark in some ways is a summarizing Gospel; but in many of the pericopae where Mark overlaps, his account is longer than the parallels, a tendency that seems to belie the "digest" character of his Gospel. As an example, note Mark 5:1–20 pars.

arguments are not new, but they help us to see why many students of the Gospels have argued that Luke did not know Matthew, nor is there good reason to think that Mark is the last Gospel in the Synoptic sequence.

Other arguments for Luke's nonuse of Matthew exist.[14] First, Luke does not reproduce the typically Matthean additions within the triple tradition. What is in mind here are not individual terms, which sometimes do appear, but longer additions (like the exception clauses in the divorce pericope, or Jesus' remarks to Peter after his confession). None of these longer units appears. Second, why does Luke lack the longer Beatitudes section of the Sermon or the longer form of the Lord's Prayer if they were standing in front of him? Third, why does Luke rarely insert material from the double tradition into the same Markan context as Matthew (3:7–9, 17, and 4:2b–13 are the only exceptions)? The degree of Luke's disagreement with Matthean order is an argument developed below. These arguments summarize briefly the macro arguments that raise questions about whether Luke used Matthew.

One final argument comes strictly from order. Here I produce a chart that deals with pericopae sequence from Luke 3:1–9:50. This is where one can compare the bulk of triple-tradition texts, outside any possible influence from texts tied to the Passion account, whose source history may be more complex. In this chart, Luke appears in the middle position, since it is his use we are concerned to examine. Both Mark and Matthew appear to try to show their relationship to the Lukan sequence. The chart asks the reader to consider both Matthew and Mark in the first position. Which Gospel looks to fall more naturally in a position Luke used?[15]

---

14. A more complete treatment is that of Joseph A. Fitzmyer, *The Gospel according to Luke I–IX,* AB 28A (Garden City, N.Y.: Doubleday, 1981), 73–75.

15. Remember that those who hold to the Griesbach hypothesis will argue that Mark followed Luke and thus the careful practice of Peter's interpreter explains the lack of disruption in the sequence between Luke and Mark. An * means that a jump in sequence has taken place other than a reversal of proximate pericopae. Other shifts in order that proceed for more than one unit are indicated by [].

Pericopae Sequence for Matthew-Luke-Mark
(Luke 3:1–9:50)

Topic	Matthew	Luke	Mark
John the Baptist	3:1–6	3:1–6	1:2–6
John's preaching	3:7–10	3:7–9	—
Crowd's question	—	3:10–14	—
One to come	3:11–12	3:15–18	1:7–8
John in prison	[14:3–4]	3:19–20	[6:17–18]
Jesus' baptism	3:13–17	3:21–22	1:9–11
Genealogy	[1:1–17]	3:23–38	—
Temptations	4:1–11	4:1–13	1:12–13
Journey to Galilee	4:12	4:14a	1:14a
In Galilee	4:13–17	4:14b–15	1:14b–15
Luke lacks Matt. 4:18–22 // Mark 1:16–20			
Nazareth synagogue	[13:53–58]	4:16–30	[6:1–6a]
Capernaum synagogue	—	4:31–32	1:21–22
Demoniac at synagogue	—	4:33–37	1:23–28
Peter's mother-in-law	*8:14–15	4:38–39	1:29–31
Sick healed	8:16–17	4:40–41	1:32–34
Departs Capernaum	—	4:42–43	1:35–38
First preaching tour	[4:23]	4:44	1:39
Catch of fish	—	5:1–11	—
Cleansing of leper	[8:1–4]	5:12–16	1:40–45
Paralytic	*9:1–8	5:17–26	2:1–12
Levi (Matthew)	9:9–13	5:27–32	2:13–17
Fasting	9:14–17	5:33–39	2:18–22
Sabbath grain	*12:1–8	6:1–5	2:23–28
Withered hand	12:9–14	6:6–11	3:1–6
Choosing Twelve	[10:1–4]	6:12–16	3:13–19
Multitudes healed	4:24–25 // 12:15–18	6:17–19	[3:7–12]
Sermon: beatitudes	5:3–12	6:20–23	—
Sermon: woes	—	6:24–26	—
Sermon: love	5:38–48	6:27–36	—
Sermon: judging	*7:1–5	6:37–42	[4:24–25?]
Sermon: fruit	*7:15–20 // 12:33–35	6:43–45	—
Sermon: house/rock	7:21–25	6:46–49	—
Centurion	[8:5–13]	7:1–10	—
Widow at Nain	—	7:11–17	—
John the Baptist's question	*11:2–6	7:18–23	—

Topic	Matthew	Luke	Mark
Jesus on John	11:7–19	7:24–35	—
Sinful woman	—	7:36–50	—
Ministering women	—	8:1–3	—
Sower	*13:1–9	8:4–8	4:1–9
Reason/Parables	13:10–17	8:9–10	4:10–12
Interpretation of sower	13:18–23	8:11–15	4:13–20
He who hears	—	8:16–18	4:21–25
Jesus' family	[12:46–50]	8:19–21	[3:31–35]
Storm stilled	*8:23–27	8:22–25	*4:35–41
Gerasene demoniac	8:28–34	8:26–39	5:1–20
Jairus/woman	*9:18–26	8:40–56	5:21–43
Twelve commissioned	*10:1, 7–11, 14	9:1–6	*6:6b–13
Herod's opinion	[14:1–2]	9:7–9	6:14–16
Apostles' return	*14:12b–13	9:10a	*6:30–31
Five thousand fed	14:13–21	9:10b–17a	6:32–44
Luke's "Great Omission" of Mark 6:45–8:26			
Peter's confession	*16:13–20	9:18–21	*8:27–30
Passion prediction #1	16:21–23	9:22	8:31–33
Come after me	16:24–28	9:23–27	8:34–9:1
Transfiguration	17:1–9	9:28–36	9:2–10
Matthew and Mark share Elijah question Luke lacks			
Boy exorcized	*17:14–21	9:37–43a	*9:14–29
Passion prediction #2	17:22–23	9:43b–45	9:30–32
Greatness	[18:1–5]	9:46–48	9:33–37
Exorcism permitted	[10:42]	9:49–50	9:38–41

A survey of the chart shows that there is far more dislocation with the Matthean pericopae than with the Markan. It must be said that this chart does not prove the case for Luke's use of Matthew, as some suggest. Redaction would allow for pericopae to be rearranged according to thematic needs. However, the chart does raise a plausible argument to an important level. Should we really believe that it is inherently more likely that Luke bounced around Matthew as the chart suggests rather than that he paralleled Mark as consistently as the chart suggests? Given what we seem to know about Luke's care in handling his tradition, the better argument internally seems to reside with a use of Mark and not of Matthew.

So this brings us to the key point of our discussion. How, then, do we explain some 225 verses primarily of Jesus' teaching that Matthew and Luke share if Luke did not know or use Matthew?[16] It is here that Q's existence is posited to explain this amount of textual data. Could this agreement be explained on the basis of independent tradition? As we shall see, the argument for Q rests on issues of both wording and order, though the case for about two-thirds of this collection of texts is stronger than for the remaining third. For example, a look at Matt. 3:7b–10 and Luke 3:7b–9 shows all but four words agreeing with one another, including word sequence, which in Greek can be varied while retaining the same meaning. Other texts show similar, significant verbal agreement (Matt. 3:11–12 par.; Matt. 4:1–11 par.; Matt. 7:3–5 par.; Matt. 11:2–11 par.; Matt. 11:16–19 par.; Matt. 8:18–22 par.; Matt. 11:20–24 par.; Matt. 11:25–27 par.; Matt. 7:7–11 par.; Matt. 12:22–30 par.; Matt. 12:43–45 par.; Matt. 12:38–42 par.; Matt. 6:22–23 par.; Matt. 6:25–34 par.).[17] Thus, the case for Q, even though it is a posited source, is plausible based on the internal evidence of the biblical text. Now the question becomes, What is Q's character?

The Character of Q

The examination of Q's character has always surfaced key themes in the material. The classic study goes back to T. W. Manson, *The Sayings of Jesus*.[18] He divided the Q material into four basic groups and used the Lukan versification to identify the units, as has become common: (1) John the Baptist and Jesus (3:7–9, 16–17; 4:1–13; 6:20–49; 7:1–10; 7:18–35); (2) Jesus and his disciples (9:57–62; 10:2–3, 8–16; 10:21–24; 11:2–13); (3) Jesus and his opponents (11:14–26; 11:27–28; 11:29–36; 11:42–52; 12:2–3;

16. This argument works, even if one argues that Mark was the first Gospel. When Mark is placed first, one still has to explain where all this agreement came from if Luke did not use Matthew.

17. For a handy synopsis of Q text candidates laid out in English-Greek diglot, see John S. Kloppenborg, *Q Parallels: Synopsis, Critical Notes and Concordance* (Sonoma, Calif.: Polebridge, 1988).

18. This work was published in 1949 and had an earlier form in 1937 as *The Mission and Message of Jesus*. *Sayings* was reissued by SCM Press in 1959. Citations in this essay are from that edition.

12:4–12, 22–34); and (4) the future (12:35–59; 13:18–21; 13:22–30, 34–35; 14:15–24; 14:25–27, 34–35; 16:13, 16–18; 17:22–37).[19] The first section treats Jesus' relationship to John and some of Jesus' basic teaching as an introduction to the collection. The second treats aspects of discipleship and mission. The third focuses on his controversies with Israel, while the fourth deals with eschatology and issues tied to the return of the Son of man.

A more recent study by Dale Allison shows how things have both changed and remained the same.[20] He presents five sections of material. His first section matches Manson's on John and Jesus. His second section also agrees with Manson's second, "Jesus and the Disciples," except that Allison includes 11:2–4 here, a text Manson expands in his list to 11:2–13. Allison notes how this section appears addressed to those sent out in mission. Allison's third section, "Controversies with Israel," is also close to Manson's third section, only adding 13:34–35 and omitting 12:4–12, 22–34. At this point, Allison goes his own way with a short fourth section that could be titled "The Father's Care for His Own" (12:2–12, 22–32), a unit Manson included in the opponents section as evidence of persecution concerns. Allison also has a large fifth section composed of a combination of parables, passages on division and persecution, and eschatological texts of practical advice and exhortation (12:33–34, 35–40, 42–46 [47–48?], 49–53, 54–56, 58–59; 13:18–19, 20–21, 23–24, 25–27, 28–30 + 14:11; 14:16–24; 26; 27; 34–35; 14:4–7; 16:13; 16–17; 18; 17:1–4; 6; 22:37; 19:12–26; 22:28–30). The different and varied character of this last section is obvious. It contains many more short, aphoristic units. The listing does seem to suppress some decidedly key longer eschatological units (12:35–40; 17:22–37; 19:12–26), which may suggest the abiding value of Manson's appeal to a distinct fourth section tied to eschatology in Q.[21]

19. Lukan versification has become the standard method of citation because the belief is that Luke has preserved the basic order of Q materials. See Manson, *Sayings*, 14–15. For these lists, see his table of contents.

20. Dale Allison, *The Jesus Tradition in Q* (Harrisburg, Pa.: Trinity, 1997).

21. Allison (*Jesus Tradition*, 27–28) challenges the appeal to the future for these texts, arguing that some passages, like 14:27, 34–35; 15:4–7; 16:13; and 16:18 do not treat the future, but are a part of the units. The criticism is correct for those texts, but all it may suggest is that the "future" section of material is smaller than Manson suggested.

One other new feature surfaces in Allison's approach that shows a shift in how Q has been treated in the last few decades. Allison and other more recent Q critics like to discuss the history of Q's composition. They tend to speak of material in basic theme categories, such as wisdom, eschatology, and mission, and then suggest that Q possessed one of these themes originally and saw the others added as time passed. This type of discussion surrounding Q has been a staple of recent study.[22]

It is here that Q studies seems to reach beyond what can really be demonstrated. Though the basic themes of introduction to Jesus' teaching alongside John, exhortations to mission alongside wisdom teaching, and eschatology seem well established, the assumption that Q or a collection like it needed to work on only one theme at a time is precisely that—an assumption that cannot be established. Since this "one theme only" premise underlies the attempts to assess the history of Q's composition, it is evident that if that assumption is faulty, so are all of these thematic analyses. Is it a given that the collection of a Jesus tradition would only be interested in topics one dimension at a time, especially when none of the traditions we do have limit themselves in this way? It is here, though I think a good case can be made for Q, that I think serious questions must be raised about the possibility of actually getting

22. Major studies, besides Allison's, made different cases for the sequence. Siegfried Schulz (*Q: Die Spruchquelle der Evangelisten* [Zürich: Theologischer, 1972]) argues that the apocalyptic strand was the oldest, followed by wisdom, Son of God Christology, and concerns about the delay of the return in a later stage. Athanasius Polag (*Die Christologie der Logienquelle*, WMANT 45 [Neukirchen-Vluyn: Neukirchener, 1977]) placed John the Baptist, wisdom themes as seen in the Sermon on the Plain, and mission themes as the earliest elements. Other elements came in two later stages. Migaku Sato (*Q und Prophetie: Studien zur Gattungs- und Traditionsgeschichte der Quelle, Q* WUNT 2.29 [Tübingen: Mohr-Siebeck, 1988]), argues for the primacy of the prophetic themes alongside the material on Jesus and John. John Kloppenborg (*The Formation of Q: Trajectories in Ancient Wisdom Collections*, SAC [Philadelphia: Fortress, 1987]) has produced the most influential study in the American context. It argues for the primacy of the more wisdomlike material of community-directed exhortation. Later came the prophetic-apocalyptic materials. Sato's study is really a major challenge to Kloppenborg, showing how bound together wisdom and apocalyptic are in many texts, making a separation of such themes difficult. Allison (*Jesus Tradition*, 4–8) has a telling critique of Kloppenborg. An insightful treatment of current discussion is that of Ronald A. Piper, "In Quest of Q: The Direction of Q Studies," in *The Gospel behind the Gospels: Current Studies on Q*, ed. Ronald A. Piper, NovTSup 75 (Leiden: Brill, 1995), 1–18.

behind the texts that we have. Even if Q was assembled in stages, how can we really determine their order or how early the pieces were assembled? It seems that such studies, though worth pursuing as possibilities for Q's development, must be seen to be what they are: exercises dependent on sufficient speculation that any results lack a solid enough foundation on which to build any superstructure. It is this element of Q studies, the pursuit of its compositional history, that leads to the abuse of Q in New Testament studies, a topic to which I shall return later.

Thus, I have suggested that the character of Q, as far as its content goes, highlights three basic themes: (1) introducing Jesus alongside John, (2) mission and wisdom exhortation for disciples, and (3) eschatology. This means that the spectrum of teaching in Q treats ideas as varied as Son of man Christology and judgment, to loving one's enemy in the midst of mission and persecution.

One other set of important observations about Q needs attention. These relate to the order of the Synoptic use of the material and the extent of agreement in the wording of the material. For reasons of space, I can only be suggestive here. A check of a synopsis will show that the order of proposed Q material in Matthew and Luke in the first two sections of Allison's listing tends to follow a fairly consistent sequence within both Matthew and Luke, with exceptions easily explained along redactional lines. It is also the case that many of these texts possess the most extensive verbal agreement.[23] What the agreement in both wording and order suggests is that these passages from Q are the best established and supply the best evidence for being part of a fixed document or tradition. However, when one ventures into the remaining sections of Q, this consistency involving both order and wording significantly diminishes, especially in the "catch-all" fifth section of Allison's listing. It is here as well that settings for these sayings vary greatly along with the wording. This is so much the case that some people like to speak of Matthean-Q and Lukan-Q or of a "stream of common tradition" versus a fixed document. It is also in this fifth section that the shortest and most concise sayings appear, often with a significant variation of wording.

23. For a list of these texts, see the previous section and the discussion tied to note 18 and the treatment of Manson. For a summary chart of "core Q texts," see appendix 2.

Some of this can be attributed to redaction, but again a question begs for an answer: Why are these texts less consistently rendered than other portions of Q? A plausible reply may be that these sayings existed in some variation and in multiple points of the early church tradition, possibly because they were the types of things Jesus taught regularly. Thus, some "Q" texts in these materials may not be from Q alone. This factor may account for the differences. Such a reply wreaks havoc on precise Synoptic study. In fact, B. S. Easton admitted as much in trying to defend a single document, saying that a single document cannot be proved but "it is wholly likely, particularly as dividing into two or more documents simply leads to needless complexity."[24] This is no counterargument, especially when we know that oral tradition was an extant element of the early church culture.

What I am arguing is that although one can make a case for Q's existence and define the key elements of its character, its compositional history is likely to remain a mystery to us. This is because the nature of our textual evidence and the inherent complexity of the early tradition with its mixture of textual and oral sources makes tracing the exact lines of Q's history next to impossible short of the discovery of a Q document itself. So, one question remains: How do we use Q? With that question comes a corollary: What about the abuse of Q? To these topics I now turn.

The Use and Abuse of Q

The use of Q emerges directly from what we can and cannot know about the likely source. Again my remarks are brief and suggestive.

Those Q texts that show extensive verbal agreement and that appear in similar contexts in Matthew and Luke can and should be evaluated as part of a tradition that had solid roots in the early church and as reflective of Jesus' teaching. The preservation of these materials is a sign of the respect that the church had to pass on these teachings.[25] As I shall suggest later, the collection of texts in Q became less necessary to preserve when the Gospels incorporated them so completely into their "apostolic" accounts.

24. *The Gospel according to St. Luke* (New York: Scribner, 1926), xx.
25. See appendix 1 for a sample of the range of such texts: two similar and two dissimilar.

More difficult is the assessment of Q material that comes in significantly altered verbal form or appears in widely divergent contexts in Matthew and Luke. Here numerous factors need consideration before assuming that Q is the only possible source for this material. First, is the teaching in question of such a proverbial character or so concise that it could have been preserved in various settings, as well as taught on various occasions? It is parabolic and aphoristic sayings that tend to fall into this category. Thus the parable of the talents/minas (Matt. 25:14–30; Luke 19:11–27) may be not one parable reworked by a second Gospel writer, but two distinct parables told with some variation. Second, is the contextual relocation of a given Gospel a reflection of an evangelist's own topical and anthological arrangement, so that the different context is merely a redactional move? The use of the parables of the mustard seed and leaven (Matt. 13:31–33; Luke 13:18–21) may belong in this category. What Matthew presented as a section on kingdom parables, Luke spread out to indicate how Jesus taught about the kingdom periodically. Many texts in Q could be the result of either of these diverse factors. It is often the case that one cannot be sure about such judgments, so any conclusions about the tradition history of such units need to be held tentatively.

Also helpful is the reminder that Jesus' relationship to John, the mission of disciples (especially to Israel), the ethics of the disciples, and their need to depend on God in the face of rising opposition are themes that reach into the very heart of Jesus' earthly ministry, not merely themes tied to a specific community. We need to remember that the only "evidence" we possess for making such judgments about contextual setting and the history of tradition is what we find in our texts and the comparisons we can make between those passages. All other judgments about setting and community are inferences made about the evidence and not solid evidence itself.

Perhaps the place where Q material is most abused is in the picking and choosing between the age and original sequence of the source's themes. One has the sense that preferences do not emerge from the nature of the evidence, but on the basis of some preconceived view of how the tradition developed. Even if one can separate strands of concerns—and that does seem somewhat possible—it is next to impossible to discern the order of those strands and say anything definitive about when they might have been brought together or by whom. It is not self-evident that texts about mission must belong to a setting distinct from wisdom or apocalyptic concerns. We should be especially skeptical of community-specific solutions to such questions, as if Jesus' public teaching and discipleship instruction emerged only to address extremely limited community concerns.

This brings us to the issue of the abuse of Q. It is here that efforts like those popularized by the Jesus Seminar should receive a just rebuke as poor historiography at a time when they are catching intense media attention. When Burton Mack appeals to the glitz of a "lost Gospel Q" as the basis for an earliest Christianity that was devoid of eschatology, high Christology, or judgment themes, as well as passion or resurrection accounts, the study of Q has crossed into historical revisionism and distortion.[26] Even what little we have in Jewish tradition about Jesus tells us that what made his ministry an offense to the Jewish leadership had to do with far more than any wisdom teaching.[27] Jesus' actions and challenge of the law had to raise issues tied to his person and authority. Authority questions were at the heart of the conflict.[28] Something about Jesus had to fuel the eschatological fervor evident in all strands of the tradition we do possess. Something had to fuel the messianic confession of the early church that also inspired the charge on his cross to read, "Jesus of Nazareth, King of the Jews."

26. Burton L. Mack, *The Lost Gospel: The Book of Q and Christian Origins* (San Francisco: HarperCollins, 1993).

27. For a survey of such texts, see F. F. Bruce, *Jesus and Christian Origins outside the New Testament* (Grand Rapids: Eerdmans, 1974).

28. Even a host of moderate works on the historical Jesus do not draw the lines of demarcation in anywhere near the absolute terms of these "lost Gospel" works. I have in mind here John Meier, *A Marginal Jew: Rethinking the Historical Jesus*, 2 vols., ABRL (New York: Doubleday, 1991–94), or Ben F. Meyer, *The Aims of Jesus* (London: SCM, 1979), which are but two examples. Works like those by Mack argue that the earliest communities are defined in categories emerging from Q and the *Gospel of Thomas*, quickly dismissing the Christology of Mark as fueled by early church myth and relegating most of the rest of the Synoptic tradition to historical irrelevancy. Not only does this make the alleged Q community almost distinct in its emphases, but it also elevates what is in all likelihood a second-century, gnostically influenced Gospel (*Thomas*) to an importance out of proportion with its historical location. For treatment of such questions from a conservative viewpoint, see Michael Wilkins and J. P. Moreland, eds., *Jesus under Fire: Modern Scholarship Reinvents the Historical Jesus* (Grand Rapids: Zondervan, 1995).

If the retort comes that we cannot be sure that such a detail is accurate, nor even the charge it represents, then we might as well confess that we know next to nothing about the real Jesus from the passion accounts in the Gospels, as they are our only sources about those events. No reconstructions can help us if our sources are this poor. The line between historical reconstruction and revisionism is pretty thin when one rejects even the most basic elements of the story line from the sources. All of a sudden there are lots of gaps into which one can place almost anything plausibly connected to the ancient world and only selectively connected to our sources. This kind of "divide and conquer" strategy is popular in the most culturally attractive forms of modern New Testament criticism. It allows our culture to embrace (if that is a good word) a culturally acceptable but theologically emasculated Jesus whose challenges extended only to differences in approach and in his greater openness to others without seriously engaging the issue of his authority to make such claims or changes. In a premodern culture, where religion was central to identity and often sought to mark persons as in or out, some critics' modern or postmodern Jesus is really a contemporary square peg trying to be squeezed into an ancient round hole, a mismatch of the worst kind.[29]

Even more, a tradition-history of Q that argues that this original community was nonmessianic and noneschatological must explain the likelihood of the alleged later messianic and eschatological community using so many texts from a community that lacked so many features that the emergent community now embraced as fundamental. Can we really believe that the alleged development would be so smooth and noncontroversial that the emergent messianic community, holding to a high Christology, would accept the teachings of a group that held to Jesus as merely a prophetic teacher of wisdom, especially when its own traditions rejected that prophetic portrait as too limited a view of Jesus? If later doctrinal controversy over Christology is any guide, then we can reasonably doubt the plausibility of such a historical reconstruction.

29. It is not hard to imagine what this kind of religiously fueled culture is like, for many of the less technologically sophisticated cultures in our present world reflect how contentious such religious dialogue is.

My point is that the acceptance of Q's existence does not carry with it the corollary that one must accept all that has been attached to Q's existence or origin(s) by biblical criticism. What we know about Q is very limited. In addition, what some have speculated about the origins of Q looks to be wrong, not only going beyond what evidence we do possess, but also requiring a historical reconstruction that cannot stand as credible.

Conclusion

Source criticism is an exercise in discernment about the nature of both our external and internal evidence about the Gospels. I have argued that there is a likelihood that a second source to Matthew and Luke included a document like Q. I regard that as more likely than that Matthew was the first Gospel or that Luke used Matthew, given the nature of the ambiguity of the external evidence about Matthew's origin and issues of content and order between Matthew and Luke. However, I have questioned whether all that is called Q can be shown to have its source in a single document. While a substantial portion of this material may come from such a source, enough variation exists that we must reckon with the likelihood of the influence of other sources, whether written or oral. This means we must speak more cautiously about the history of tradition in Gospel materials and in given passages involving possible Q texts than we tend to do.

I have also questioned whether our internal evidence is good enough to "unpack" the history behind or underneath this Q source. I think we can know what we have, but can be less certain of tracing its exact history.

Finally, I have questioned the use of this material by some critics who are too confident, in my view, that the wisdom elements preceded the other emphases found in Q. Such work seems excessively speculative and requires a historical reconstruction of the relationship between various stands of the early church that is hardly credible. It allows them to pitch a Jesus who never spoke about who he was or about ultimate accountability to God. The lack of the theme of accountability to God would be unprecedented, even for a prophetic figure, much less an eschatological-messianic one. This Jesus is unoffensive to our public religion and discourse, with its desire to accept multiple ways to God. So it is on the surface an attractive portrait of Jesus, especially in a culture that is becoming less acquainted with the Gospel sources about him. However, this "Jesus of wisdom" is an incomplete portrait of his ministry and has little correspondence to the Jesus who was so offensive that the Jewish and Roman leadership executed him. Such uses of Q are really abuses of what we can know about the source and about Jesus.

In sum, my advice is to refer to Q and recognize its testimony to fundamental themes of Jesus' teaching used by the early church. It serves as a major witness to what Jesus taught about John, mission-ethics-persecution, as well as eschatology and judgment. It seems possible to identify much of its content. However, use it cautiously, paying attention to both wording and sequence as you think about it as a source. Realize that what Q represents, if it did once exist, is an indication of respect for certain key themes in Jesus' teaching that the source came to pass on. That material became so incorporated into our Gospel material that its full presence there becomes the likely explanation for Q's disappearance, unless, of course, the Griesbach view of Gospel sequence is correct. In that case, only my remarks about the abuse of Q stand. In that scenario, however, one will then be discussing the abuse of Matthew, not Q.

As I argue for Q, I realize that it is but one piece of the larger Gospel puzzle. My case for its existence is the product of various judgments made along the way about the Gospels. Perhaps it is of some comfort in the midst of the debate about Gospel sequence that one thing both views can affirm is that the earliest Christianity is not to be found in the sum of Q plus *Thomas*.[30] For the earliest Christianity, who Jesus was and what he taught was made up of far more than what we see in Q, as the rest of what we have in the fourfold Gospel powerfully shows. Whatever questions we have about Q and whatever resolution we contend for about those questions, may the church never lose sight of the fact that its mission is to focus upon and proclaim the Jesus whom the combination of our sources reveal. Tragically, this is a Jesus whom the world is rapidly losing sight of, in

30. William R. Farmer (*The Gospel of Jesus*) poses this argument with rhetorical power from a Griesbachian perspective.

part because of the work of revisionists who have abused the likely presence of Q. In other words, whether one argues for the presence of Q or of Matthew followed by Luke, let us not forget that the real subject is Jesus. He is the source whose existence is ultimately responsible for the sources we do have.

Appendix 1: Comparison of Sample Q Texts

The following sample texts show the range of similarity and dissimilarity in selected texts often associated with Q. For the full range of texts, one can check either *Q Parallels* by John Kloppenborg or Frans Neirynck's *Q Synopsis*. The Greek text is the 27th ed. of Nestle-Aland. The first two samples are very similar, while the last two are quite diverse. Boldface type indicates verbal agreement, though word order has been ignored. Variant forms of the same term are not noted. For these agreements, see Kloppenborg. Remember that determining presence in Q is often a function of theme and contextual placement as well as verbal or conceptual familiarity. The last two examples are but two of several that many question as being a part of Q because of the vast array of differences.

Matthew 3:7–10 and Luke 3:7–9

Matthew 3:7–10: Ἰδὼν δὲ πολλοὺς τῶν Φαρισαίων καὶ Σαδδου-καίων ἐρχομένους ἐπὶ τὸ βάπτισμα αὐτοῦ εἶπεν αὐτοῖς· γεννήματα ἐχιδνῶν, τίς ὑπέδειξεν ὑμῖν φυγεῖν ἀπὸ τῆς μελλούσης ὀργῆς ποιη-́σατε οὖν καρπὸν ἄξιον τῆς μετανοίας καὶ μὴ δόξητε λέγειν ἐν ἑαυ-τοῖς· πατέρα ἔχομεν τὸν Ἀβραάμ. λέγω γὰρ ὑμῖν ὅτι δύναται ὁ θεὸς ἐκ τῶν λίθων τούτων ἐγεῖραι τέκνα τῷ Ἀβραάμ. ἤδη δὲ ἡ ἀξίνη πρὸς τὴν ῥίζαν τῶν δένδρων κεῖται· πᾶν οὖν δένδρον μὴ ποιοῦν καρπὸν καλὸν ἐκκόπτεται καὶ εἰς πῦρ βάλλεται.

Luke 3:7–9: Ἔλεγεν οὖν τοῖς ἐκπορευομένοις ὄχλοις βαπ-τισθῆναι ὑπ᾽ αὐτοῦ· γεννήματα ἐχιδνῶν, τίς ὑπέδειξεν ὑμῖν φυγεῖν ἀπὸ τῆς μελλούσης ὀργῆς; ποιήσατε οὖν καρποὺς ἀξίους τῆς μετα-νοίας καὶ μὴ ἄρξησθε λέγειν ἐν ἑαυτοῖς· πατέρα ἔχομεν τὸν Ἀβραάμ. λέγω γὰρ ὑμῖν ὅτι δύναται ὁ θεὸς ἐκ τῶν λίθων τούτων ἐγεῖραι τέκνα τῷ Ἀβραάμ. ἤδη δὲ καὶ ἡ ἀξίνη πρὸς τὴν ῥίζαν τῶν δένδρων κεῖται· πᾶν οὖν δένδρον μὴ ποιοῦν καρπὸν καλὸν ἐκκόπτε-ται καὶ εἰς πῦρ βάλλεται.

Matthew 11:25–27 and Luke 10:21–22

Matthew 11:25–27: Ἐν ἐκείνῳ τῷ καιρῷ ἀποκριθεὶς ὁ Ἰησοῦς εἶπεν· ἐξομολογοῦμαί σοι, πάτερ, κύριε τοῦ οὐρανοῦ καὶ τῆς γῆς, ὅτι ἔκρυψας ταῦτα ἀπὸ σοφῶν καὶ συνετῶν καὶ ἀπεκάλυψας αὐτὰ νηπίοις· ναὶ ὁ πατήρ, ὅτι οὕτως εὐδοκία ἐγένετο ἔμπροσθέν σου. Πάντα μοι παρεδόθη ὑπὸ τοῦ πατρός μου, καὶ οὐδεὶς ἐπιγινώσκει τὸν υἱὸν εἰ μὴ ὁ πατήρ, οὐδὲ τὸν πατέρα τις ἐπιγινώσκει εἰ μὴ ὁ υἱὸς καὶ ᾧ ἐὰν βούληται ὁ υἱὸς ἀποκαλύψαι.

Luke 10:21–22: Ἐν αὐτῇ τῇ ὥρᾳ ἠγαλλιάσατο [ἐν] τῷ πνεύματι τῷ ἁγίῳ καὶ εἶπεν· ἐξομολογοῦμαί σοι, πάτερ, κύριε τοῦ οὐρανοῦ καὶ τῆς γῆς, ὅτι ἀπέκρυψας ταῦτα ἀπὸ σοφῶν καὶ συνετῶν καὶ ἀπεκάλυψας αὐτὰ νηπίοις· ναὶ ὁ πατήρ, ὅτι οὕτως εὐδοκία ἐγένετο ἔμπροσθέν σου. πάντα μοι παρεδόθη ὑπὸ τοῦ πατρός μου, καὶ οὐδεὶς γινώσκει τίς ἐστιν ὁ υἱὸς εἰ μὴ ὁ πατήρ, καὶ τίς ἐστιν ὁ πατὴρ εἰ μὴ ὁ υἱὸς καὶ ᾧ ἐὰν βούληται ὁ υἱὸς ἀποκαλύψαι.

Matthew 18:12–14 and Luke 15:4–7

Matthew 18:12–14: Τί ὑμῖν δοκεῖ; ἐὰν γένηταί τινι ἀνθρώπῳ ἑκατὸν πρόβατα καὶ πλανηθῇ ἓν ἐξ αὐτῶν, οὐχὶ ἀφήσει τὰ ἐνενήκοντα ἐννέα ἐπὶ τὰ ὄρη καὶ πορευθεὶς ζητεῖ τὸ πλανώμενον; καὶ ἐὰν γένηται εὑρεῖν αὐτό, ἀμὴν λέγω ὑμῖν ὅτι χαίρει ἐπ᾽ αὐτῷ μᾶλλον ἢ ἐπὶ τοῖς ἐνενήκοντα ἐννέα τοῖς μὴ πεπλανημένοις. οὕτως οὐκ ἔστιν θέλημα ἔμπροσθεν τοῦ πατρὸς ὑμῶν τοῦ ἐν οὐρανοῖς ἵνα ἀπόληται ἓν τῶν μικρῶν τούτων.

Luke 15:4–7: τίς ἄνθρωπος ἐξ ὑμῶν ἔχων ἑκατὸν πρόβατα καὶ ἀπολέσας ἐξ αὐτῶν ἓν οὐ καταλείπει τὰ ἐνενήκοντα ἐννέα ἐν τῇ ἐρή-μῳ καὶ πορεύεται ἐπὶ τὸ ἀπολωλὸς ἕως εὕρῃ αὐτό; καὶ εὑρὼν ἐπιτίθησιν ἐπὶ τοὺς ὤμους αὐτοῦ χαίρων καὶ ἐλθὼν εἰς τὸν οἶκον συγκαλεῖ τοὺς φίλους καὶ τοὺς γείτονας λέγων αὐτοῖς· συγχάρητέ μοι, ὅτι εὗρον τὸ πρόβατόν μου τὸ ἀπολωλός. λέγω ὑμῖν ὅτι οὕτως χαρὰ ἐν τῷ οὐρανῷ ἔσται ἐπὶ ἑνὶ ἁμαρτωλῷ μετανοοῦντι ἢ ἐπὶ ἐνενήκοντα ἐννέα δικαίοις οἵτινες οὐ χρείαν ἔχουσιν μετανοίας.

Matthew 10:34–36 and Luke 12:51–53

Matthew 10:34–36: Μὴ νομίσητε ὅτι ἦλθον βαλεῖν εἰρήνην ἐπὶ τὴν γῆν· οὐκ ἦλθον βαλεῖν εἰρήνην ἀλλὰ μάχαιραν. ἦλθον γὰρ δι-χάσαι ἄνθρωπον κατὰ τοῦ πατρὸς αὐτοῦ καὶ θυγατέρα κατὰ τῆς μητρὸς αὐτῆς καὶ νύμφην κατὰ τῆς πενθερᾶς αὐτῆς, καὶ ἐχθροὶ τοῦ ἀνθρώπου οἱ οἰκιακοὶ αὐτοῦ.

Luke 12:51–53: δοκεῖτε ὅτι εἰρήνην παρεγενόμην δοῦναι ἐν τῇ γῇ; οὐχί, λέγω ὑμῖν, ἀλλ᾽ ἢ διαμερισμόν. ἔσονται γὰρ ἀπὸ τοῦ νῦν πέντε ἐν ἑνὶ οἴκῳ διαμεμερισμένοι, τρεῖς ἐπὶ δυσὶν καὶ δύο ἐπὶ τρισίν, διαμερισθήσονται πατὴρ ἐπὶ υἱῷ καὶ υἱὸς ἐπὶ πατρί, μήτηρ ἐπὶ τὴν θυγατέρα καὶ θυγάτηρ ἐπὶ τὴν μητέρα, πενθερὰ ἐπὶ τὴν νύμφην αὐτῆς καὶ νύμφη ἐπὶ τὴν πενθεράν.

Appendix 2: Order of Core Q Texts

This listing follows Allison's first two groupings. The consistency in group 1 texts is slightly clearer than in group 2. However, it is often suggested that Matthew may have brought together teaching material into an anthology representative of Jesus' teaching in his discourse groupings. These would show up in the sermon and in the mission discourse. This might explain some of the dislocations.

Luke	Matthew
1. Jesus-John and Basic Ministry	
3:7–9	3:7–10
3:16–17	3:11–12
4:1–13	4:1–11
6:20–49 (sermon)	5:3–12
	5:38–48
	7:1–5
	7:15–20
	7:21–27 (sermon)
7:1–10	8:5–13
7:18–35	11:2–6
	11:7–19
2. Jesus and His Disciples	
9:57–62	8:18–22
10:1–16 (mission)	9:37–38
	10:7–16
	11:20–24
	10:40 (mission)
10:21–24	11:25–27
11:2–4	6:9–13 (sermon)
11:9–13	7:7–11 (sermon)

3

A GENERATION WHO KNEW NOT STREETER

The Case for Markan Priority

Scot McKnight

Introduction

Each generation of scholars learns contemporary scholarship and learns it well. Gospel scholars today know the names of John Kloppenborg and J. P. Meier and J. D. Crossan and N. T. Wright; they know a smattering of Judaism as embedded in the scholarship of J. Neusner or E. P. Sanders; they know about source criticism from W. R. Farmer and his students; they know about textual criticism from Kurt Aland; they know New Testament theology from . . . well, there aren't any new ones to read so they don't know that much about New Testament theology. They know Matthew from W. D. Davies and D. C. Allison Jr., Mark from R. H.

I wish here to express my appreciation to David Black, and any others involved in the administration of Southeastern Baptist Theological Seminary, for the kind invitation to participate in the New Testament Symposium.

Gundry, and Luke from J. Fitzmyer or D. Bock or J. B. Green, and John from R. E. Brown. Today's students know these names.

The unfortunate, however unintended, implication of coming to grips with modern scholarship is that in learning contemporary scholarship, students put the previous generation on the shelf. These scholars are sitting there full of chat, but, sadly, modern students don't have time for older studies, and so the books become forlorn as the faces of the scholars become lonely, sad, and unknown. It is a fact that modern scholarship's improvements do not necessarily make older scholarship obsolescent.

Three features of modern scholarship have been a major force in the decline of learning the scholarship—especially that of B. H. Streeter—connected with one of the most intriguing puzzles of modern scholarship: the Synoptic problem. First, the rise of deconstructionist projects has called into question the pursuit of truth as well as the legitimacy of traditional historical knowledge. Harold Bloom once said that nothing good came out of the '60s; I think the same about the recent trends swirling around deconstructionism. That's because these scholars don't say much about the author or about truth, but instead they talk about themselves, about readers, about power, and about the modern world's *Angst*. I can't take seriously people who speak of *Angst* in deriving meaning from a text while they write texts that they think have lots of meaning and a transparent intention to subvert meaning. They specialize in knowing that we can't know, and they particularly like telling others that they can't know what they think they know. Alvin Kernan, in his deservedly notable book, *In Plato's Cave*, in which he writes his memoirs of the shifts of modern education in the second half of the twentieth century, says that they "took uncertainty to its nihilistic extremes in the humanities and social sciences, 'demystifying' traditional knowledge, replacing positivism with relativism, substituting interpretation for facts, and discrediting objectivity in the name of subjectivity."[1] As Edward Shils, the famous soci-

---

1. Alvin Kernan, *In Plato's Cave* (New Haven: Yale University Press, 1999), xvi. One should also read in this connection R. Scholes, *The Rise and Fall of English: Reconstructing English as a Discipline* (New Haven: Yale University Press, 1998).

ologist and education scholar at the University of Chicago, once said, "This has been a hard century . . . for truth."[2]

The one person the deconstructionists don't know about is B. H. Streeter, and that is too bad for them. His book is tidy and bloated with Greek words in rococo detail, and assumes all the time that when we read a text, we've got a pretty good idea of what it says. He knows that when he comes to a sign that says "Stop," it really isn't open to audience and reader response. He grinds his wheels to a full stop. He also knows a lot about the early church and about the Synoptic problem, in fact, a lot more than Augustine and Origen knew, and that is why young students should read Streeter.

In speaking here of Streeter, however, let me add an important clarification that emerged from my conversations with Professor Farmer in the sitting room of the Manor House at Southeastern Baptist Theological Seminary. I don't think that Streeter solved the Synoptic problem permanently, nor do I believe that Streeter is without need of improvements. In fact, scholarship since Streeter has modified his arguments and rejected others. So, when I am speaking of Streeter, I am speaking here of the Oxford hypothesis (see below) with its refinements. In particular, I am speaking of Christopher Tuckett,[3] and others like him, who hold to Markan priority as stated by Streeter but refined since. I still consider Streeter's book important to the discussion, and not just for historical reasons, but because he formulates arguments on the basis of a careful sifting of the evidence of the Synoptic Gospels. If we might reshape the language of his conclusions, he nonetheless had his finger on data.

Second, and unfortunately, the curriculum that follows the deconstructionist trend also follows the narrative critics. They, too, don't care about Streeter or the Synoptic problem, but for different reasons. Streeter and other Synoptic-problem scholars think that you can't understand a text accurately unless you know its context and its tradition-history. The narrative critics think that the text *is* the context. This, I believe, is a mistake, but

---

2. E. Shils, *The Calling of Education: The Academic Ethic and Other Essays on Higher Education* (Chicago: University of Chicago Press, 1997), 120.

3. *The Revival of the Griesbach Hypothesis: An Analysis and Appraisal,* SNTSMS 44 (Cambridge: Cambridge University Press, 1983).

it surely makes learning scholarship easier: you don't have to read the old books, because they mistakenly believed that texts don't have contexts; rather, they have textual clues, and if you read carefully (which means following the latest trend of narrative criticism), you will see all you need to see. And if we look hard enough, once again, we will find the *Angst*.

Since I have not been asked to tell stories about narrative critics and deconstructionists but instead to talk about why I think Mark is the first Gospel, I will move on to that. But my point is still the same: modern students don't know the Oxford hypothesis, and that spells trouble for Markan priority in the days ahead. And there is the third reason why students today don't read Streeter: W. R. Farmer. Professor Farmer and his students are about the only ones talking about the Synoptic problem, and they've got the ear of lots of students. They have been saying since the mid–1960s that we shouldn't accept any more wooden nickels, and they think Streeter minted several. A sense of confusion occurs among students when they see scholars like David Dungan and Christopher Tuckett bump their chests against one another and then each thump his chest in victory. Students hear these debates and conclude that we can't know. It takes courage to take a firm stand on the Synoptic problem, and our students are often not that courageous, so they choose other games to play.

So here is where we are: deconstructionists tell us not to worry about such things as the Synoptic problem, because we can't know truths about history; narrative critics tell us that it doesn't matter, because texts tell us all we need to know; and Farmer and his students are telling us that Markan priority is wrong—and our students get intimidated by the whole endeavor. My worry is manifest now: methodologies subvert interest in the Synoptic problem while only a handful of scholars are discussing what I consider to be a significant historical and exegetical gateway into theological perception. And that handful rarely has a voice from the side of the Oxford hypothesis.

In what follows, I examine the modern debate, the phenomena of the Synoptic Gospels, and the Oxford hypothesis itself, and then I proceed to state the arguments for that theory along with some of its problems. My time on the campus of Southeastern revealed to me two things: first, that the debate about the Synoptic problem is thriving on some campuses, and second, that at

Southeastern at least, the vast majority seem to prefer the Griesbach hypothesis. If I begrudgingly admit that I am glad to see the
issues being discussed and the evidence trotted out, I am also
aware that theories like this can take on an inordinate place as a
test of "orthodoxy" for some groups. I echo, therefore, the comments of my friends, Craig Blomberg and Darrell Bock, that one's
view of the Synoptic problem transcends one's theological commitments. In particular, adherence to the Oxford hypothesis is no
more a sign of liberal persuasion (as if nineteenth-century German or early-twentieth-century English scholarship always got
things wrong) than adherence to the Griesbach hypothesis is a
visible sign of commitment to conservative orthodoxy (as if the
traditional view always gets things right). This is an issue that
needs to be hammered out on the anvil of Gospel evidence and
not shaped by a priori theological persuasions.

The Modern Debate

Professor Blomberg has provided a very nice survey of names
and positions, so I need only highlight certain dimensions of
this debate in what follows. Of the more notable recent developments in the Synoptic problem, two deserve mention here. The
first is the revival of the Griesbach hypothesis, largely due to the
pressing and persistent questions of Professor W. R. Farmer as
well as the recondite subjects of his students' various works. Because of the persuasive and administrative designs of Farmer
(and other Griesbach proponents), there have been at least five
major international conferences that have taken up the Synoptic problem in a serious forum.[4]

However, the revival of the Griesbach hypothesis has not been
unchallenged. In 1979 C. M. Tuckett successfully defended a Ph.D.
dissertation on the Griesbach revival, and an abbreviated version

4. A survey of these conferences, with listings of major papers and partici-
pants, can be found in W. R. Farmer, ed., *New Synoptic Studies: The Cambridge
Conference and Beyond* (Macon, Ga.: Mercer University Press, 1983), vii–xxiii.
The list of Dungan is complete, though the significance of each is not discussed.
See D. L. Dungan, *A History of the Synoptic Problem: The Canon, the Text, the
Composition, and the Interpretation of the Gospels*, ABRL (New York: Doubleday,
1999), 375–78.

of this dissertation followed.[5] Tuckett concludes that the Griesbach hypothesis is not as satisfactory a solution to the Synoptic problem as the Oxford hypothesis. Tuckett's studies are very good and judicious, even if they are filled with technical scuttlebutt.

Inside the circles of Farmer is David Laird Dungan, who has undertaken, after decades of study, a complete history of the Synoptic problem. I consider his book, with some criticisms mentioned below, to be the most significant book on the Synoptic problem since Farmer, outside the work of Christopher Tuckett. Rethinking the entire issue for decades has opened up the lens of Dungan to four factors involved in the Synoptic problem: (1) textual criticism—which text is used; (2) canon—which books are authoritative; (3) composition—how the Gospels were created; and (4) hermeneutics—how the Gospels are interpreted. Dungan's insights are legion, and it is a pity we cannot detail all of them here. From among them I include the following: (1) the importance of Tatian, Origen, and Augustine in the shaping of the questions; (2) the weight of Spinoza's diatribes against the Dutch and European political and theological establishments; (3) the inclusion of political and economic issues in the debate about biblical interpretation; (4) the influence of W. R. Farmer on the revival of the Griesbach hypothesis.

Because space does not permit a full review, nor is this essay intended to be a review of the Griesbach hypothesis, I need to mention several problems I find in reading Dungan, though these criticisms do not diminish in any substantial way the major lines of his thinking. The first influences the whole history of the Synoptic problem: the move from Tatian to Origen and then on to Augustine, in which the priority of Matthew becomes "orthodoxy," is not subjected to serious criticism. The development is noted and traced, with important insights that have not always been noted, but that evolution is not subjected to evaluation. In fact, one might say that there is one conclusion to draw on the basis of Dungan's discussion (though he does not state this as I do): the rise of Matthean priority in this period was never established by carefully comparing Synoptic texts. Instead, when Eusebius issued his canons, he took the most popular Gospel, Matthew,

---

5. *The Revival of the Griesbach Hypothesis: An Analysis and Appraisal,* SNTSMS 44 (Cambridge: Cambridge University Press, 1983).

and put it first, and that is far too much of the story. Augustine's arguments were never serious arguments; he did not carefully compare the three Synoptics to see which might be the first. Instead, he used Eusebius's canons and tried to show that Mark and Luke, or later (if David Peabody is right, and he may be) Luke and Mark, can be historically conformed to Matthew or at least historically confirmed as accurate history.[6] Augustine's gift to the church was at the level of historicity, not at the level of careful exegesis of the phenomena of the Synoptic problem.

Second, I don't think that Dungan is evenhanded in his history. But let me state that I almost sympathize with his approach—the Oxford hypothesis has been given so much attention and so thorough a credence that the alternatives have been given short shrift. Nonetheless, the reader needs to know that Griesbach is given a saint's decoration while Streeter is dressed down to rags; Farmer is wearing full regalia while Tuckett is wearing the emperor's new clothes! The rise of the Griesbach hypothesis today is given lots of fireworks,[7] especially in the contributions of Farmer and Dungan himself (whose contributions are notable indeed), but hardly any attention is given to the work of Christopher Tuckett, who has ably and famously responded to the Griesbach proponents. In fact, he has at times clarified their arguments and created a more peaceful environment in which we now work together. He has given in to arguments from their side and has refined the arguments significantly. But in Dungan's account, Tuckett gets mentioned in the

6. The study by David Peabody was questioned at the conference, though no consensus was reached. When I asked both David Dungan and W. R. Farmer why it was that no one picked up on this supposed revision by Augustine, neither had an explanation (though I do not think one is fundamentally necessary, nor do I think Peabody is wrong because no one before him saw what he sees now). In other words, the earlier (Book 1) theory of Matthew-Mark-Luke became the only theory connected with Augustine, though Peabody thinks Augustine later revised this to be Matthew-Luke-Mark in Book 4. See his "Augustine and the Augustinian Hypothesis: A Reexamination of Augustine's Thought in *De consensu evangelistarum*," in Farmer, ed., *New Synoptic Studies*, 37–64.

7. For a collection of comments, see P. M. Head, *Christology and the Synoptic Problem: An Argument for Markan Priority*, SNTSMS 94 (Cambridge: Cambridge University Press, 1997), 5–6.

text without substance three times and then he gets about one page when Dungan is talking about recent developments.

Along with this slanted historical account, Dungan sets up the reader with a major kind of expectation that I don't think is met: in particular, Dungan goes to some lengths to show the political and economic agendas involved in Spinoza and John Locke, but when he gets to the Synoptic problem, we don't see how the Germans or Sanday's seminar were influenced by politics and economics. Let me put this sharply: while Dungan is happy to find political and economic motives behind the advance of the historical-critical method as it was to emerge forcefully in Markan priority, he seems to forget those agendas when it comes to Griesbach and Farmer, and he neglects to explore its implications in the special case of the British and the growing consolidation of Markan priority. I wish Dungan had gone on to a more comprehensive set of factors influencing both Streeter (if also Tuckett) and Farmer (as well as the modern American Griesbach theorists).

My final problem with Dungan strikes at the heart of what I consider to be a significant factor in the history of Christian scholarship. I was disappointed with Dungan's appropriate castigation of German scholarship's anti-Semitic tendencies but inappropriate implication that somehow the view favoring Markan priority was to be similarly classed.[8] This takes a massively serious issue—the presence of anti-Semitism in German scholarship—and uses it emotionally to cast dark shadows over the view of Markan priority. Dungan then suggests, admittedly with no evidence, that the Third Reich favored Markan priorists. Let me say that I am not suggesting Dungan is wrong when he says that some German scholars were anti-Semitic; and neither would I be surprised to find that some German scholars let anti-Semitism influence their judgments on the priority of Matthew. (No evidence is offered, but we shouldn't be naïve about that period of scholarship.) Moreover, I am sure that David Dungan is not suggesting that all Markan prioritists are influenced by that sort of judgment. Moreover, I am also sure that David Dungan does not think Markan priorists are anti-Semitic. But he leaves this issue quite open and shouldn't have. Griesbachians might

8. Dungan, *History*, 339–40.

feel that Dungan has made an important point; as a Markan prioritist who has publicly denounced anti-Semitism, all I can say is that I feel that Dungan is here exploiting a moral agenda for comparatively trivial conclusions. I have read the pertinent two pages over and over to see if I might have misread Dungan; I feel that I have not, and I must record here my disappointment.[9]

I suggest that Dungan would do better if he made the motive-finding dimensions of his work less conspicuous, even if he must call attention to them. While no one would want to deny that each of us has motives, including Dungan (his mistaken understanding of Gordon Fee's epistemology is a case in point), we are on the road together, and the only thing we can really argue about is the evidence that matters. Politics and economics might influence our reading of the evidence, but it is our hope that we can shed those motives often enough to find the evidence and talk about it. If we can't shed our motives and our prejudices, we might as well play the last hole and go home. Before I proceed, however, I want to say again that Dungan's book will become a standard textbook for years to come on the history of the discussion. If I wish that he had given more attention to Tuckett and had not turned to the anti-Semitic argument as he did, I also am grateful to Dungan for the painstaking care he has shown in sorting out the issues and various attempts at resolution.

Before turning to the crucial data, let me mention in passing a second area in the modern debate that deserves more attention than it has been given: how these authors would have used other books and how they wrote books and how they passed on traditions. Long ago, William Sanday published what was a "one and only" piece on the nature of writing and using sources in the ancient world: "The Conditions under which the Gospels were written, in their bearing upon some difficulties in the Synoptic Problem."[10] And the subject of how

9. The solution of Markan priority was fashioned, in fact, prior to the Third Reich, so how the Third Reich dealt with the matter is a separate issue. I should, however, record the observation that the issues that emerged in the diabolical Third Reich consciousness had a history prior to that time, but Dungan does not trace that development.

10. Essay no. 1 in *Oxford Studies in the Synoptic Problem* (Oxford: Clarendon, 1911).

ancients wrote was only lightly touched upon later when Bruce Metzger penned his essay on tables and desks.[11] Then F. Gerald Downing published four finely researched articles on how the ancients used their sources, articles that throw some weight toward the Oxford hypothesis.[12] The discussion has been carried forward significantly and insightfully by Sharon Lea Mattila and also somewhat more by A. R. Millard.[13] The phenomenon of writing and using sources was quite unlike our modern methods of stacking books on our desk, or writing down quotations on cards, or having assistants run things down so we can bloat our notes, or having a CD-ROM that accesses data instantaneously—in short, our procedures did not exist back then, and we may be in constant need of reminding ourselves of this difference. The consensus of these scholars is that ancients read their materials (read: sources) and then basically seemed to land firmly on one source and use it with supplementation from others; and that use of the original source was often by appeal to "short-term memory" (read it, set it down—on a table or in a cylinder—write a new text).[14] I make two applications: the use Matthew made of Mark, as found in Robert H. Gundry's redactional eruditions, and the so-called "zigzag" approach of Griesbach proponents, each surrenders to the same criticism—they don't consider carefully enough the phenomenon of writing.[15] Other phenomena now need to be examined.

11. "When Did Scribes Begin to Use Writing Desks?" in *Historical and Literary Studies: Pagan, Jewish, and Christian*, NTTS 8 (Grand Rapids: Eerdmans, 1968), 121–37.

12. F. G. Downing, "Compositional Conventions and the Synoptic Problem," *JBL* 107 (1988): 69–85; "A Paradigm Perplex: Luke, Matthew and Mark," *NTS* 38 (1992): 15–36; "Redaction Criticism: Josephus' Antiquities and the Synoptic Problem: I," *JSNT* 8 (1980): 46–65; "Redaction Criticism: Josephus' Antiquities and the Synoptic Problem: II," *JSNT* 9 (1980): 29–48.

13. S. L. Mattila, "A Question Too Often Neglected," *NTS* 41 (1995): 199–217; A. R. Millard, "Writing and the Gospels," *QC* 5 (1995): 55–62.

14. Along a similar line, though working at the issue of how the Gospels came into existence as canonical texts, see Ulrich Victor, "Was ein Texthistoriker zur Entstehung der Evangelien sagen kann," *Bib* 79 (1998): 499–514.

15. Darrell Bock mentioned to me that he thinks that the recent studies on Luke by Farmer's students may suffer from the same weakness.

The Phenomena of the Synoptic Gospels

I begin by observing that our Synoptic Gospels (Matthew, Mark, and Luke), when carefully compared in a synopsis,[16] show some remarkable signs of similarity along with even more interesting cases of dissimilarity. The evidence we find in underlining our synopses is just that: phenomena in need of a good explanation. There are several of these patterns in the evidence that need to be explained. What matters here is both a discovery of the phenomena and a judicious examination of that evidence to see if anything in the evidence makes us lean one way or the other. Let me also say that this evidence is labyrinthine in connection and endless in density.

The first matter is the *phenomenon of content:* the evangelists record similar events and sayings of Jesus. In fact, approximately 90 percent of Mark is found in Matthew and approximately 50 percent of Mark is found in Luke. Furthermore, approximately 235 verses, mostly sayings of Jesus, are common to Matthew and Luke but are not found in Mark.[17] This set of facts—and it is an intricate, inextricable, and malleable set of data—permits several explanations: one might argue that Matthew used Mark or that Mark used Matthew (with all sorts of permutations); one might argue that they both used an *Urgospel.* This evidence is important, but nothing definitive for a proof emerges from the observation that the Synoptics have a dramatically similar content.

16. One of Dungan's most important contributions is his analysis of how the choice of a synopsis influences one's perspective (*History*, 332–37). There are several good synopses available. The standard, critical synopsis of the Gospels is K. Aland, *Synopsis Quattuor Evangeliorum*, 10th ed. (Stuttgart: Deutsche Bibelgesellschaft, 1978). Because this synopsis contains no English translation, many students prefer K. Aland, *Synopsis of the Four Gospels*, 7th ed. (New York: United Bible Societies, 1984). Other good synopses include A. Huck and H. Greeven, *Synopsis of the First Three Gospels* (Tübingen: Mohr, 1981 [available from Eerdmans]); B. Orchard, *A Synopsis of the Four Gospels in Greek: Arranged According to the Two-Gospel Hypothesis* (Macon, Ga.: Mercer University Press, 1983); R.W. Funk, *New Gospel Parallels*, 2 vols. (Philadelphia: Fortress, 1985). For a survey of the history of making synopses, see R. H. Stein, *The Synoptic Problem: An Introduction* (Grand Rapids: Baker, 1987), 16–25.

17. This is commonly referred to as "Q," the first letter of the German word *Quelle*, meaning "source."

Second, the *phenomenon of order* describes the simple fact that at least two of the Evangelists agree almost all the time on the order of the events in the life of Jesus. An example may be observed by beginning at Matt. 17:22–23; Mark 9:30–32; Luke 9:43b–45. The next event is found only in Matthew (17:24–27). Then a common order is resumed: Matt. 18:1–5; Mark 9:33–37; Luke 9:46–48. Though Matthew does not record the next incident, both Mark and Luke do (Mark 9:38–41; Luke 9:49–50). Again, two are united on the next event (Matt. 18:6–9; Mark 9:42–50). The point is simple: two evangelists almost always agree on the matter of order. Again, various explanations can be offered: Matthew used Mark or Mark used Matthew (with various other options available). But one important conclusion emerges from the phenomenon of order: the Synoptic Gospels are most probably connected at the literary level. I include here an *Urmarcus* theory but do not have it in mind. Whether first or third, Mark is the middle factor when it comes to the argument from order. We have, again, no proof, but we do have an important conclusion.

Third, we come to the *phenomenon of words*. If, to take but one example from the double tradition, one compares the wording of Matt. 3:7–10 and Luke 3:7–9 in parallel columns, one observes substantial similarity. (Similarity appears as single underscore; dissimilarity as a double underscore. Translations are from the NASB.)

Matthew 3:7–10	Luke 3:7–9
But when he saw many of the Pharisees and Sadducees coming for baptism, he said to them,	He therefore began saying to the multitudes who were going out to be baptized by him,
"You brood of vipers, who warned you to flee from the wrath to come?	"You brood of vipers, who warned you to flee from the wrath to come?
Therefore bring forth fruit in keeping with repentance; and do not	Therefore bring forth fruits in keeping with repentance; and do not
suppose that you can say to yourselves,	begin to say to yourselves,
'We have Abraham for our father';	'We have Abraham for our father';
for I say to you that God is able from these stones to raise up children to Abraham. And the axe is already laid at the root of the trees; every tree therefore that does not bear good fruit is cut down and thrown into the fire."	for I say to you that God is able from these stones to raise up children to Abraham. And also the axe is already laid at the root of the trees; every tree therefore that does not bear good fruit is cut down and thrown into the fire."

Observe how this statement by John (Matt. 3:7b–10; Luke 3:7b–9) is repeated by two authors in nearly identical language. The Greek text, apart from the introductory statements, shows only three variations, indicated by a double underscore: (1) whereas Matthew has "fruit" (3:8), Luke has "fruits" (3:8); (2) whereas Matthew has "do not suppose that you can" (3:9), Luke has "do not begin to" (3:8); (3) Luke has the added "also" (3:9). These differences do not count for much. Various explanations of these empirically observable phenomena might be offered: Luke copied Matthew, or Matthew copied Luke, or each copied another source (Q), or God told both of them the same thing. Phenomena, but no necessary conclusion.

Where are we, then? We are reasonably confident that Matthew, Mark, and Luke are related at the literary level and that it is highly likely that they are mutually dependent, however one might see that relationship or set of relationships. We are also reasonably confident that Mark is the middle factor. Is there any kind of argument that permits any higher level of probability? I think so, but before I proceed to that argument I need here to sketch the Oxford hypothesis.

The most enduring and influential theory of how these phenomena ought to be explained is the Oxford hypothesis. What I will do here is state the basics of the Oxford hypothesis before offering an evaluation. I am aware that my descriptor, "Oxford hypothesis," is not the normal one. More often the solution is called the "two-source hypothesis," and the Griesbach solution the "two-Gospel hypothesis." These are good terms, but I don't use them. I think something is gained when we use "Oxford hypothesis": we grab the solution at its most definitive stage and furthermore at the stage that has become most influential. Today, most who believe in Markan priority do so because of B. H. Streeter's presentation, not because of what H. J. Holtzmann or K. Lachmann argued. They continue to believe in that theory, if they care to think about it, because of its more recent refinements under the hand of Christopher Tuckett.

The Oxford Hypothesis

When William Sanday organized his famous seminar on the Synoptic problem in 1894, which convened three times per term until 1910, the dominant solution to the Synoptic problem in England seems to have been the "oral hypothesis."[18] For approximately fifteen years students and friends of Sanday, including J. C. Hawkins,[19] B. H. Streeter, and W. C. Allen,[20] gathered periodically to go through a synopsis paragraph by paragraph. The discussions were eventually brought to fruition in an influential volume, *Studies in the Synoptic Problem by Members of the University of Oxford.*[21]

The singularly most influential source critic of Sanday's Oxford seminar is B. H. Streeter, who, thirteen years after Sanday's *Studies* was published and upon further reflection, completed the definitive work that expounded the Oxford hypothesis.[22] Though scholars have criticized Streeter and modified his views here and there, it cannot be said that any one work on the Synoptic problem has had more influence than his. In brief, Streeter contended that there were four sources involved in the making of the Synoptic Gospels, and, he maintained, both their dates and provenance can be discerned:

1. Q, those verses common to Matthew and Luke but not in Mark, was composed in Antioch in approximately A.D. 50.
2. L, the original source for Luke's Gospel, was written in approximately A.D. 60 in Caesarea.

18. For example, one can consult the standard work of B. F. Westcott, *An Introduction to the Study of the Gospels,* 8th ed. (London: Macmillan, 1895), 165–212, esp. 192–212, where Westcott puts each current theory to the test. It is clear that Sanday himself was dependent on the German scholar H. J. Holtzmann; see W. R. Farmer, *The Synoptic Problem: A Critical Analysis* (Dillsboro, N.C.: Western North Carolina Press, 1976), 51–63.

19. See especially his *Horae Synopticae: Contributions to the Study of the Synoptic Problem,* 2nd ed. (Grand Rapids: Baker, 1968). On Hawkins, see the statements of S. C. Neill, *The Interpretation of the New Testament, 1861–1961* (London and New York: Oxford University Press, 1964), 126–27.

20. Famous for his ICC volume on Matthew, a commentary singularly concerned with source-critical matters: *A Critical and Exegetical Commentary on the Gospel according to St. Matthew,* 3d ed. (Edinburgh: T. & T. Clark, 1912).

21. Ed. W. Sanday (Oxford: Clarendon, 1911).

22. B. H. Streeter, *The Four Gospels: A Study of Origins, Treating of the Manuscript Traditions, Sources, Authorship, and Dates* (London: Macmillan, 1924). For further details about Streeter, see Neill, *Interpretation,* 131–36.

3. M, the source for the special material in Matthew, was written in Jerusalem in approximately A.D. 60.
4. Mark was written in A.D. 66 in Rome.
5. The combination of Q and L was made by Luke, a companion of Paul, and the resultant document Steeter called "proto-Luke."
6. Our canonical Luke is the result of conflating proto-Luke with a special source for Luke 1–2 and the Gospel of Mark; this was accomplished in approximately A.D. 80, perhaps in Corinth.
7. Matthew wrote his Gospel in approximately A.D. 85 in Antioch, and he did so by combining Mark, Q, M, and what Streeter called the "Antiochene Tradition."[23]

What has survived from this complex hypothesis, admittedly with dimensions that are from time to time challenged,[24] is more accurately called the Oxford hypothesis, which states that there were at least two written sources: Q and Mark. Few today would contend that there was a written source M or L; fewer still adhere to the proto-Luke hypothesis.[25] Nonetheless, in spite of its weaknesses, the essential theory of B. H. Streeter won the day, and to this day, again with appropriate revisions, garners the majority of scholars. The theory, no matter how deeply rooted it is in German scholarship, owes its definitive form to the work of Sanday's seminar.[26] To deny Streeter's importance and give credit exclusively to modern proponents is analogous to excluding the original writers of the U.S. Constitution and giving sole credit to the current supreme court justices (and this analogy might get way out in the sea before breaking up).

23. Streeter's famous chart can be found on p. 150.
24. Streeter was hit hardest for suggesting order and date for these hypothetical sources. In short, he "knew too much" because he inferred more than the evidence allowed.
25. See R. P. Martin, *The Four Gospels*, vol. 1 of *New Testament Foundations: A Guide for Christian Students* (Grand Rapids: Eerdmans, 1975–78), 152–56, for a sympathetic discussion.
26. It is a criticism of both B. Reicke (*The Roots of the Synoptic Gospels* [Philadelphia: Fortress, 1986]) and E. Linnemann (*Is There a Synoptic Problem? Rethinking the Literary Dependence of the First Three Gospels*, trans. R. Yarbrough [Grand Rapids: Baker, 1992]) that they too narrowly describe the two-source hypothesis (Oxford hypothesis) from its German roots.

Arguments for Markan Priority

So far we have established, on the basis of the three phenomena (content, order, wording), that the Synoptics are related to one another. We have also argued that there are various explanations of the three phenomena. Is there anything that can adjudicate the matter?[27] Anything that can function as an actual proof? Since Professor Bock has the assignment of arguing for Q, which is part of the Oxford hypothesis, I confine my comments to Markan priority.

David Peabody, an expert in Synoptic problem methodological issues, has expressed it accurately when he points to the linguistic data:

> The issue is not whether any particular literary evidence can be interpreted as consistent with a source hypothesis. The issue is whether there are linguistic phenomena within the Synoptic gospels which have decisive value for solving the Synoptic Problem—data which would unambiguously indicate the direction of literary dependence between any two of the three Synoptic Evangelists.[28]

I begin right here for the sole logical foundation for any solution to the Synoptic problem. The Oxford hypothesis is more probable because of the *linguistic phenomena*. Put simply, the linguistic phenomena of the Synoptic Gospels can be more easily explained if Mark is seen as prior to both Matthew and Luke than if Mark is seen as a later conflation of Luke and Matthew.[29] I emphasize here "more easily explained" and do not say "can only be explained."

27. Farmer (*Synoptic Problem*, 227–32) is one of the few who self-consciously works out methodological features of priority. See now Head, *Christology*, 28–48.

28. D. B. Peabody, "Chapters in the History of the Linguistic Argument for Solving the Synoptic Problem: The Nineteenth Century in Context," in *Jesus, the Gospels, and the Church: Essays in Honor of William R. Farmer*, ed. E. P. Sanders (Macon, Ga.: Mercer University Press, 1987), 61.

29. The best listing of these can be found in Hawkins, *Horae Synopticae*, 131–38, and deals with odd Markan elements that are not found in the parallels in Matthew and Luke; these include unusual words and constructions (thirty-three examples), incomplete sentences (thirteen examples), and omission of conjunctions (twenty-one examples).

So far as I can see, the Griesbach proponents have not dealt with the most decisive argument favoring the Oxford hypothesis: the argument from the more original reading.[30] The most telling argument against the Griesbach hypothesis and for the Oxford hypothesis is the accumulated answers to this question: Which reading most likely gave rise to the other readings? Put differently, given Matthew's (or Luke's) rendering of a saying or event, is it likely that Mark is a later rendition of Matthew or Luke (or both), or is it more likely that Mark is the source for the others?[31] The answers so consistently move in the direction of Markan priority that one is compelled either to adopt the Oxford hypothesis or jettison text-critical procedures in use by all scholars today.[32]

In fact, the recent analysis of the text-critical argument by M. C. Williams, one of my doctoral students when I was at Trinity, establishes such an argument.[33] After analyzing the Markan apparatus in NA[27] to establish the kinds of features that characterize posteriority in variant readings, Williams then compares Mark to Matthew to see if the same kinds of changes characterize Matthew's relationship to Mark. His conclusions are threefold: (1) the kinds of readings in Mark's apparatus are the kinds of readings in Matthew when compared to Mark; (2) text-critical arguments clearly and consistently support Markan priority

30. The most careful linguistic work to date from a Griesbach hypothesis viewpoint is that of Farmer's student, D. Peabody, *Mark as Composer*, NGS 1 (Macon, Ga.: Mercer University Press, 1988). But Peabody's work is surprisingly disappointing in conclusions regarding the Synoptic problem. I know of no thorough response to the kind of linguistic phenomena pointed out by Hawkins, *Horae Synopticae*, 114–53. Consequently, the language factor remains the Achilles heel for the Griesbach hypothesis. Professor Farmer informed the audience and presenters during his session at the symposium that in fact this work is presently being done by some Griesbach proponents.

31. This is the classic argument put forward in convincing fashion by J. Fitzmyer in "The Priority of Mark and the 'Q' Source in Luke," in *Jesus and Man's Hope*, 2 vols. (Pittsburgh: Pittsburgh Theological Seminary, 1970), 1:131–70, esp. 134–47.

32. See D. R. Catchpole, *The Quest for Q* (Edinburgh: T. & T. Clark, 1993), 4.

33. Matthew C. Williams, "Is Matthew a Scribe? An Examination of the Text-Critical Argument for the Synoptic Problem" (Ph.D. diss., Trinity Evangelical Divinity School, 1996). This study, of course, builds on the very important article by Gordon Fee, "A Text-Critical Look at the Synoptic Problem," *NovT* 22 (1980): 12–28.

and Matthean posteriority; and (3) those who use the Nestle-
Aland text should also, to maintain consistency, conclude for
Markan priority when compared to Matthew. Though the work
of Williams is available only through UMI Dissertation Services,
his is the only study in the history of the discussion that methodologically examines the Markan apparatus for the kinds of
changes actual scribes made to Mark and then examines Matthew's differences to see if the Matthean differences are like the
scribal changes. His conclusion is that Matthew sometimes was
a scribe using Mark (and close parallels are required to establish
this, for Matthew is more than a scribe), and this because the
changes in Matthew are like the changes made by scribes to
Mark. More objectively, when comparing the two texts, Williams concludes that the text-critical argument supports substantially Markan priority, with a few exceptions. Williams is
presently a missionary in Spain and does not have time to work
this thesis into publication form. However, he does have an article scheduled to be published by the *Journal of Higher Criticism*
that shows the influence of Owen on Griesbach. His study is important, and I hope it will be published some day.

Someone who has published a dissertation is David Peabody,
a notable proponent of the Griesbach hypothesis, and he has an
important chapter, in a Festschrift dedicated to Professor
Farmer, on the linguistic argument.[34] I need to pause for a look
at this article to see if it challenges the points I am making here.
Peabody observes that modern proponents of Markan priority,
namely, W. G. Kümmel and C. Tuckett, both claim that the linguistic argument presented by H. J. Holtzmann was decisive for
the triumph of Markan priority. According to Peabody, Holtzmann's linguistic argument (however influential) depended
upon the arguments of C. G. Wilke and E. Zeller, and Holtzmann put less weight on these arguments than is sometimes
claimed. Peabody is probably correct here. Holtzmann was using Wilke and Zeller, and the latter's arguments were far more
sophisticated. But, we ask, where does this lead us? We know
that Holtzmann was not an original thinker, and we know that
Zeller's arguments in fact were in favor of the Griesbach hypothesis. Where do these observations lead us? Do they overturn the

34. Peabody, "History of the Linguistic Argument."

linguistic argument? I will say this clearly: Peabody could be right in what he describes—that Kümmel and Tuckett are not appealing to a good source—but achieve virtually nothing in the big picture. Peabody does not draw radical conclusions from this weak appeal to ancient authorities. Knowing that Holtzmann got things disoriented affects neither the data used today for the linguistic argument nor the conclusions drawn from it.

Peabody's careful work, both in his dissertation and in his subsequent studies, illustrates what I see as a tendency of Griesbach scholarship, and I need to comment on it here: the proclivity to point out hidden motives and agendas of those who were advocating Markan priority. This ad hominem type of argument, however, proves little. We find it in Farmer's criticisms of Streeter, in Peabody's criticisms of Holtzmann, and in Dungan's criticisms of nineteenth-century German scholarship. I think that Stoldt is at the bottom of some of this, but it doesn't matter, because finding hidden motives hardly overturns the evidence even when it is the product of bad logic. Holtzmann, Sanday, and Streeter, at their worst, used specious arguments but won the day. They won the day because of the cumulative nature of their arguments.

And the foundational argument for Markan priority is the linguistic argument; it is the *only* argument with probative and decisive force. At the 1992 SBL annual meeting I spoke to the two-Gospel hypothesis seminar and addressed this very issue, the linguistic argument. David Black responded. The point I made there I make here: the Griesbach proponents have yet to come up with a counterargument to the linguistic argument. Perhaps I don't know all the scholarship produced by Griesbachians on the linguistic argument, but I can say that I haven't seen anything that even tries to address the issue. C. S. Mann's commentary on Mark in the Anchor Bible series was an attempt to do this.[35] I believe that his commentary is a failure when it comes to assessing the linguistic data. He assumes Matthean priority and then explains Markan redaction in light of it, but more often he avoids the discusson. I shall say more about this below.

35. C. S. Mann, *Mark: A New Translation with Introduction and Commentary*, AB 27 (Garden City: Doubleday, 1986).

We return to the Oxford hypothesis and the linguistic argument and how textual criticism leads to a more definitive kind of argument. I stated that those who use the Nestle-Aland text should also favor Markan priority; if they don't, then they ought to abandon the Nestle-Aland text. I say this not because the text is biased toward Markan priority—a separate and interesting question in its own right—but because the fundamental question of textual criticism is this: Which reading most likely gave rise to the other readings? I now proceed to three examples, and for each set of data I ask this question: Without presupposing an order, and supposing you found these two pieces of evidence, which do you think is more likely the original?

Example 1: Mark 7:31 and Matthew 15:29

At this point I need to give a specific example for the Synoptic problem to make the analogy clear. This is essentially a text-critical linguistic argument. Mark 7:31 records what is, by all accounts, a trip of Jesus: "And again, Jesus left the regions of Tyre and went through Sidon to the Sea of Galilee through the middle of the regions of the Decapolis." On any reading of this text, a very strange route has been followed: a trip southeast begins by going north, and gets to this southeast destination, the Sea of Galilee, through a region of cities even further southeast than the Sea itself. What is noteworthy here is that Matthew's account of this trip is much easier to follow: "And departing from there [the regions of Tyre and Sidon], Jesus came to the Sea of Galilee" (Matt. 15:29). For the purposes of the Synoptic problem, we can ask a simple text-critical question: Which reading most likely gave rise to the other? And the answer, for all text critics, would be that it is more likely that Mark gave rise to Matthew's clarification than for Mark to take this perfectly sensible statement of Matthew and make it obscure. What is at least more difficult to understand in Mark is easier to understand in Matthew. Mark is, therefore, more primitive and therefore probably prior to Matthew.

What about C. S. Mann, an avowed Griesbach proponent? Mann is aware of the problem and has the following observations (accompanied by my parenthetical comments):[36] (1) the

36. Ibid., 322–23.

"geography is impossible to reconstruct" (it's not impossible to reconstruct; it is, however, unlikely for someone to travel like this—unless you are picking up kids for a baseball game and have to rely on them for directions!); (2) Wellhausen's conjecture is probably right (here Mann is dealing with history, I suppose, rather than text); (3) it "is not as though the confusion of geography in Mark was offset by clarity in the other evangelists" (confusing me as to his overall solution to the Synoptic problem); (4) Matthew "has no reference to Tyre and Sidon, nor yet to the Ten Towns, contenting himself merely with the statement that Jesus 'departed from there and came by the Sea of Galilee' (15:29)" (why this is so, Mann does not ask—and that is, of course, the point); (5) Mark is awkward or maybe confused about geography (this he concedes); (6) maybe there are several traditions about Jesus' journey into "pagan territory" and Mark collects all the fragments; (7) when it comes to the "Notes" section, Mann says nothing about Mark 7:31 (actually, my observation). In my judgment, Mann has dropped the ball. He has avoided the linguistic evidence, thrown dust into the air, and by the time our eyes have cleared, he has vanished.

Example 2: Mark 14:3 and Matthew 26:6

A second example: Mark 14:3 has an unusual concurrence of two genitive absolutes in the same sentence; Matthew has a genitive absolute and then a finite verb (26:6). It is more likely that Matthew "corrected" (though that term can be defined inaccurately) Mark than that Mark took a perfectly normal expression and made it irregular. Mark's style is not impossible: people can have two genitive absolutes together if they want; in a flurry, they might add yet a third. But when we compare the two, it is more likely that someone would change two genitive absolutes (a more unusual construction) to one with a finite verb than take one genitive absolute and a finite verb and make two genitive absolutes—unless, of course, there were a pattern of such activity in Mark. He has but two others, Mark 6:21–22 and 8:1, so David Black tells me. Let me emphasize something here: we are not talking about possibilities but probabilities. I don't say it is impossible; I say it is less likely.

What about C. S. Mann? This time at least he enters the discussion. Here are his comments:[37] (1) Mark's choice of two genitive absolutes "is highly unusual," in part because place notes are infrequent in Mark and because 14:3a seems like an addition; (2) Lohmeyer is correct that Mark's narrative probably began with "in the house of Simon," just after this opening genitive absolute; (3) Mark got his opening genitive absolute ("when he was in Bethany") from Matthew's text. Mann's proposal, in my judgment, makes sense and is an explanation. But he does not deal with the problem of the "highly unusual" use of two genitive absolutes, nor does he explain why Mark would be adding things up front after he has constructed later expressions—Mark didn't have a computer, which permits editing like this. In other words, while Mann has an explanation—Mark took it from Matthew (I could say Matthew took it from Mark)—he skips over the difficulties involved in such an explanation, difficulties at the linguistic level.

It is more likely that Matthew saw Mark's two genitive absolutes and converted the second one into a finite verb than that Mark took Matthew's "typical" construction, dropped the proper name (Jesus), and made it more unusual by having two genitives. We are dealing with probabilities, not possibilities. I don't rule out the possibility. I ask only which is more probable.

Example 3: Mark 4:1 and Matthew 13:2

Mark 4:1 reads "the whole crowd was beside the sea on the land"; Matthew's parallel at 13:2 reads "the whole crowd stood on the beach." We have here two readings of one datum—which more probably is the more original according to text-critical reasoning? Let me say again, I do not ask, "What is possible?" but "What is more probably the original?" Mark's expression is redundant—those who are beside the sea are by necessity on the land! The only other options are "in the sea standing, sinking, or treading water" or "standing on the water"—which surely would have survived as a reading if it happened! But, as text critics would reason, the redundancy is not necessary; Matthew's more clipped expression "on the beach" is enough. Thus, Mark's reading is more original and more difficult and less refined grammatically. It is more likely, then, that

---

37. Ibid., 556.

Matthew has improved Mark than that Mark has taken a sharper expression and turned into a less clear expression. The famous D manuscript apparently made this kind of correction itself, omitting "on the land" from Mark 4:1.

These three texts and their parallels merely illustrate what is meant by the linguistic argument in a text-critical mode. Their number could be multiplied, but neither time nor necessity requires it. What we are dealing with is simply this: when we see two sets of linguistic data, we need to ask which is more likely the original. Explanations, of course, can work with either set of data. Text critics, however, on the basis of the kinds of data that show up in secondary readings, know that the kind of difference that emerges sometimes tips the balance in favor of a particular reading. It is my contention that a patient examination of an entire synopsis along these lines favors Markan priority. In the unforgettable words of B. H. Streeter, commenting on the cumulative effect of the linguistic phenomena when examining a synopsis, "How any one who has worked through those pages with a Synopsis of the Greek text can retain the slightest doubt of the original and primitive character of Mark I am unable to comprehend."[38]

38. Streeter, *Four Gospels*, 164. The next sentence, from the same page, is perhaps more frequently quoted: "But since there are, from time to time, ingenious persons who rush into print with theories to the contrary, I can only suppose, either that they have not been at pains to do this, or else that—like some of the highly cultivated people who think Bacon wrote Shakespeare, or that the British are the Lost Ten Tribes—they have eccentric views of what constitutes evidence." In spite of the rhetoric one hears here, it cannot be denied that the grammatical argument is the most important argument for the Oxford hypothesis. And, it remains a fact that the Griesbach proponents simply have not dealt with the phenomenon squarely. In 1992, at the SBL annual meeting in San Francisco, David Black and I engaged in a public discussion about this kind of argument. David's piece was published later as "Discourse Analysis, Synoptic Criticism, and Markan Grammar: Some Methodological Considerations," in *Linguistics and New Testament Interpretation: Essays on Discourse Analysis*, ed. D. A. Black, K. Barnwell, and S. Levinsohn (Nashville: Broadman, 1992), 90–98. In brief, my argument against David's paper is that while I grant that the kinds of points I make in this essay about Mark's grammar being "corrected" by Matthew or Luke do not preclude the possibility of Mark's grammar making sense, I maintain that such features, when run through the mill of text-critical arguments, more likely are primitive when compared to Matthew's and Luke's grammar. The issue is one of which is more likely to be primitive if one asks the question that a textual critic would ask. For further analysis, I point the reader again to Williams, "Is Matthew a Scribe?"

Second, the Oxford hypothesis is more probable because of the *theological phenomena*.[39] This involves the same logic of the first argument but now looked at from the angle of theology and its development. And anyone who reads the apparatus knows that this is a legitimate kind of linguistic or text-critical argument, even if the evidence is not absolutely consistent—so long ago pointed out by E. P. Sanders.[40] The notion that the text reveals theological alterations has been defended admirably in the recent monograph by Peter Head, which concludes that Markan priority is the best explanation of the christological argument.[41] One example will illustrate the point. Mark 6:5–6 states that Jesus was amazed at the unbelief of the Nazareth crowd and that Jesus was *"unable* to do any miracles there."[42] Early Christians may very well have been bothered by this statement because it could suggest the inability of Jesus, God incarnate, to do something. Such an impression, however, will not be given by Matthew. When he reports this narrative, in nearly identical terms, he states that Jesus "did not do many miracles there" (13:58). On the Griesbach hypothesis one has to come up with an explanation for why Mark would have taken a statement that in no way casts doubts on Jesus' ability (Matt. 13:58) and created a theological problem, whereas the Oxford hypothesis offers a more probable account of the phenomenon: Matthew eliminated a theological difficulty. It is more probable that Matthew erased a theological problem than that Mark created one. This kind of observation when comparing Matthew, Mark, and Luke not only lends support to the Oxford hypothesis, but also makes it the most probable hypothesis—though I do not consider impossible a Markan re-

39. A good listing can be found in Hawkins, *Horae Synopticae*, 117–25.
40. *The Tendencies of the Synoptic Tradition*, SNTSMS 9 (Cambridge: Cambridge University Press, 1969).
41. Head, *Christology*, esp. 8–27. One should also consult here B. Ehrman, *The Orthodox Corruption of Scripture: The Effect of Early Christological Controversies on the Text of the New Testament* (New York: Oxford University Press, 1993).
42. See Head, *Christology*, 66–83, who finds in this evidence sufficient ambiguity not to permit a firm conclusion. He sees Matthew's emphasis on faith and his simplification of Markan auxiliary verbs as potential explanatory arguments. Auxiliary verbs, however, are not all alike, and "unable" carries more weight than typical verbose auxiliary expressions.

dactional explanation.[43] And I am also aware of Peter Head's ambivalence about this type of argument, but I would argue this: all told, it is more likely that Mark is prior to Matthew than Matthew prior to Mark.

Other notable passages that need to be considered in this argument include Mark 1:11, 12, 32, 34, 41, 43, 45; 3:5, 21; 5:7, 9, 30; 6:3, 5, 6, 38, 48; 7:9, 24, 32–37; 8:12, 22–26; 9:12, 16, 21, 30, 33; 10:3, 14, 17–18, 21; 11:3, 13, 20; 12:32; 13:32; 14:14, 33, 58; 15:44–45.

Third, the Oxford hypothesis is more probable because of the *redactional phenomena*.[44] This argument is a variant of combining arguments one and two, but here I would urge a particular caution because in many cases this type of argument is more explanatory than logically decisive.[45] It is often argued that the consistency that has been found in either Matthew's or Luke's treatment of Mark is an argument in favor of Markan priority. In other words, the coherency of the theory is an argument in its favor.[46] This is an important point, but the limitations of this argument need to be noted before an illustration is given. This argument is really nothing more than an explanation that makes good sense of the data; it does not, however, approach the level of decisive proof for Markan priority except when that argument is buttressed comparatively by showing that the alternative redactional hypotheses are not as coherent.

43. See Head, *Christology*, 73–82.

44. On this, see S. E. Johnson, *The Griesbach Hypothesis and Redaction Criticism*, SBLMS 41 (Atlanta: Scholars, 1991).

45. A particularly insightful study of this kind of evidence can be seen in D. S. New, *Old Testament Quotations in the Synoptic Gospels, and the Two-Document Hypothesis*, SBLSCS 37 (Atlanta: Scholars, 1991).

46. This has been a major criterion for a solution to the Synoptic problem for C. M. Tuckett; see *Revival*, 9–15; "Arguments from Order," 205–13. See also J. M. Robinson, "On the *Gattung* of Mark (and John)," in *Jesus and Man's Hope*, 1:99–129, esp. 101–2: "In a generation in which the Synoptic problem has been largely dominant, the success of *Redaktionsgeschichte* ["redaction criticism"] in clarifying the theologies of Matthew and Luke on the assumption of dependence on Mark *is perhaps the most important new argument for Marcan priority*, just as perhaps the main ingredient lacking in William R. Farmer's argument for Marcan dependence on the other written Gospels is a convincing *Redaktionsgeschichte* of Mark based on that assumption." The same point is made by G. N. Stanton in his masterful survey of Matthean research, "The Origin and Purpose of Matthew's Gospel: Matthean Scholarship from 1945 to 1980," *ANRW* 2.25.3 (1984): 1,899–1,903.

The traditional redactional argument frequently assumes what it then concludes—though I would argue that if one can isolate redactional phenomena in one Gospel and then find them in another, the former would in general be given priority. I quote G. N. Stanton: "As far as Matthean scholarship is concerned, it has yet to be shown that any of the alternatives to the assumption that Matthew has used Mark and Q provide a more plausible and coherent account of Matthean redaction than the generally accepted view [Oxford hypothesis]."[47] Recent study, however, has improved the nuance of this argument so that one now finds redaction meaning larger, coherent patterns of thought in one Gospel in comparison with the other Gospels. I find this to be the most important contribution that Peter Head makes in his fine book on Markan priority; he calls it the "reformulated redactional argument." And, it ought to be noted here, he argues that the christological data of the Synoptic tradition find no instance in which the Griesbach hypothesis is the best explanation.

One example of redactional activity from Matthew will illustrate the nature of this argument. No one who reads Matthew will fail to miss the importance he places on the term "righteousness" and the concepts attached to it. It is found seven times in Matthew (3:15; 5:6, 10, 20; 6:1, 33; 21:32). In addition, examining these in a synopsis reveals that each one is nonparalleled. Thus, it appears that Matthew has consistently added the term to his sources because that term expresses what he wants to emphasize. One would have to ask then, on the Griesbach or Augustinian hypothesis, why neither Luke nor Mark ever saw any reason to use this term, or at least the concept, when using Matthew as a source. Further, one would have to provide reasons for Mark's or Luke's omission in each instance. These regular omissions of Matthew's particular emphases count very heavily in favor of Matthew having added them or being independent. Furthermore, the notion of doing God's will (i.e., being righteous) is a dominant and consistent feature of Matthew's redactional presentation of discipleship.[48] In light of the relative

47. Stanton, "Origin," 1,902.
48. See, for example, B. Przybylski, *Righteousness in Matthew and His World of Thought*, SNTSMS 41 (Cambridge: Cambridge University Press, 1980); R. Mohrlang, *Matthew and Paul: A Comparison of Ethical Perspectives*, SNTSMS 48 (Cambridge: Cambridge University Press, 1984), 7–26; S. McKnight, "Justice, Righteousness," *DJG*, 411–16.

absence of this Matthean theme in Mark and Luke and the pervasiveness of this theme in Matthew, it can be concluded that righteousness is a part of Matthew's redactional scheme. Accordingly, if one assumes Markan priority (and the existence of Q) and then examines Matthew's emphasis on righteousness and doing God's will, one finds a consistent redactional tendency on the part of Matthew. This, it is argued, fits the Oxford hypothesis; the hypothesis is coherent. Again, however, such an explanation is not a proof. One could argue, after all, that Mark had no reason to use the term.

These three arguments, along with a coherent explanation, demonstrate with a high degree of probability that Mark is prior to either Matthew or Luke. What I have suggested is that three of the original arguments used for the Oxford hypothesis—content, order, and words—are in fact only the phenomena and each is susceptible to various explanations. On the other hand, there is one kind of argument that raises the debate above the level of effective rhetorical explanations: the linguistic evidence as approached from the angle of the criteria used in textual criticism. I have given a few examples of the way this argument works. I am reasonably confident that this argument sustains the hypothesis so dominant in Gospel studies today.

Problems for the Oxford Hypothesis

We must not think, however, that the Oxford hypothesis is without its problems. Certainly, it is the foremost theory for explaining the origins and the relationship of the Synoptic Gospels, but the critique of the Oxford hypothesis in the last generation by Griesbach proponents has caused some important revisions, many of which are reflected in our previous discussion. What are the weaknesses of the Oxford hypothesis? Three major problems need to be mentioned.

First, the Oxford hypothesis has not sufficiently struggled with the *early Christian evidence* on the origins of the Gospels. It is noticeable that Sanday's seminar, as far as I know, did not deal with the patristic evidence with sufficient rigor. It just will not do for Oxford proponents to dismiss patristic evidence as tendentious or, worse yet, precritical and therefore naïve. Examination of this evidence may lead to the conclusion that the patristic evidence is mistaken, but such a conclusion ought not to be drawn without careful attention being given to the matter. I am relatively convinced, however, that after Origen and Eusebius the die had been cast and that independent thinking about these issues was not to be found. While I think that Augustine's *Harmony of the Gospels* is interesting for what it does—it is an attempt to show the historical trustworthiness of the Gospel stories and sayings—he is simply carrying on the tradition set by Origen and Eusebius. He did not sit down to ask the question that interests us.

Second, the major criticism of the Oxford hypothesis has been the observation of so-called *minor agreements of Matthew and Luke against Mark*. What are these? An "agreement of Matthew and Luke against Mark" is a term, expression, or entire incident in the life of Jesus that is related one way by Mark and in a different but identical way by both Matthew and Luke—and, assuming the Oxford hypothesis, when Matthew and Luke are unaware of each other's work. Thus, these are "coincidental, independent but identical alterations" to Mark.[49]

But the insignificance of a "minor" change becomes altogether more important when it is observed that within the space of a few verses, say in Mark, five "independent but identical" changes occur. This is more than a "minor agreement." And it must be admitted that these "minor agreements" work against the Oxford hypothesis because they suggest a literary relationship between Matthew and Luke. Griesbach proponents explain these as Markan alterations of Matthew and Luke where Luke has followed Matthew identically. Older Markan priorists appealed, quite intelligently, I think, to an *Urmarcus* or an *Urgospel hypothesis*. That is, they thought that Matthew and Luke used something like but not identical to our Mark, or that our Mark was based on something like itself. Thus, the "minor agreements" are not minor and deserve careful attention by Oxford proponents. One recent study by an Oxford proponent, C. M. Tuckett, has tackled the issue of the "minor agreements," and his work is worthy of careful atten-

---

49. Recent study has been intense. See esp. A. Ennulat, *Die "Minor Agreements": Untersuchungen zu einer offenen Frage des synoptischen Problems*, WUNT 2.62 (Tübingen: Mohr, 1994).

tion.[50] I do not have space to summarize it here. Robert Stein
has a mustached and bearded question: if the minor agreements
between Matthew and Luke supposedly evince a pre-Markan
tradition, what of the minor agreements that John has with
Matthew-Luke against Mark? He concludes this: such agreements indicate independent use of oral traditions, not priority
either of the Matthean-Lukan or Johannine traditions.[51]

A third problem for the Oxford hypothesis revolves around the
difficulties encountered in Q studies. Since Darrell Bock is direct-
ing his essay at this issue, I have avoided it, but a few problems
might be noted here. In particular, three problems stand out:
(1) problems with the original wording, (2) problems with the
original contents, and (3) problems with speculative theories. I
begin with the last. It goes without saying that some of the most
fertile and imaginative theories of Synoptic studies have been
raised by Q scholars.[52] Scholars have inferred a Q tradition, a Q
document, and a Q genre; from these hypotheses, a Q author and
a Q community have been posited; and from this, theories have
been developed about redactional layers and theological ideas of
the Q author(s) and his (their) community(-ies), even to the point
that some scholars are convinced that the Q community moved
several times. The problem is with probability—and the multipli-
cation of theories on the basis of a document that is already hypothetical does not increase one's chances of being accurate. The
opposite is the case! In fact, I suspect that many Gospel students
are put off by the speculative nature of Q scholarship.[53] I, for one,
am quite convinced that there was at least a Q tradition that

50. *Revival*, 61–75. Streeter's solution to these was "to divide and conquer."
Streeter isolated the various kinds of "minor agreements" and examined them
separately. By doing this, he avoided the serious accumulation of agreements in
a single location. See Streeter, *Four Gospels*, 293–331, and the telling criticisms
of Farmer, *Synoptic Problem*, 118–52 (though Farmer's tone is not productive).

51. R. H. Stein, "The Matthew-Luke Agreements against Mark: Insight from
John," *CBQ* 54 (1992): 482–502.

52. Recently, E. P. Meadors has taken Q scholarship to task for assuming too
great a difference between the theology of Mark and Q; see his *Jesus the Messianic Herald of Salvation*, WUNT 2.72 (Tübingen: Mohr-Siebeck, 1995).

53. A brief survey of Q studies can be found in J. Kloppenborg, *The Formation of Q: Trajectories in Ancient Wisdom Collections* (Philadelphia: Fortress,
1987), 8–40. What will strike most readers is that some of the studies on Q are
solid pieces, whereas others are too speculative to be probable.

can be reasonably separated from our present Synoptic Gospels, but I am deeply suspicious of any theories that go much beyond the level of identifying the general contents and wording of such a tradition. To speak, then, of a Q redactor or a Q community strikes me as too speculative to be of use. Granted, these things are not impossibilities, but they are so highly speculative that we are best left with suggestions.

And further problems arise when we try to determine the original wording of Q. Did Q have "Spirit" or "finger" of God (cf. Matt. 12:28; Luke 11:20)? And wording is not the only problem. Will it ever be possible for modern scholars to approach probability on the original contents and even the order of this hypothetical document? Connected to this is the problem that many find in Q scholarship: a theme or a formal feature (prophetic utterance, narrative) is equated with a layer and absolute consistency in a theme marks a layer. The question many of us have asked is this: Was any ancient Jewish or Christian writer absolutely consistent in this manner with themes? And, cannot different themes be used together and in different ways by one author? Thus, cannot the earliest edition of Q have had a complex relationship of wisdom and eschatology just as it had at the final layer?

For these reasons it is impossible to determine with certainty or high probability the original contents, wording, and order of Q.[54] In spite of these problems, scholars of the Oxford hypothesis have come to a fairly unanimous conclusion regarding the probable shape and contents of Q—it must not be supposed that it is all up for grabs. However, though the general contents are fairly agreed upon, it is when we need precision that we must admit that we do not have certain results.

It is not possible to evaluate carefully the other theories that were mentioned above. Virtually all scholars today fit either into the Griesbach or Oxford hypothesis. And arguments for either of these are arguments contrary to the other theories.

---

54. Since Streeter there have been several major treatments of the original order of Q. These are surveyed by Kloppenborg, *Formation of Q*, 64–80.

Conclusions

First, let me say that there is no solution, Oxford or Gries-bach, that is absolutely clear. Any theory, in fact, that explains everything easily and convincingly is overdoing it.

Second, I conclude with a firm handshake with Streeter and Tuckett on the probability of Markan priority and the existence of a Q source to which both Matthew and Luke had access.

Third, I also conclude with a simple warning: if the Markan priorists don't get busy, and if we, as a collective group, neglect to respond to the deconstructionists and narrative critics, there will come a day when we will have students who not only don't know Streeter, but also have not heard of a synopsis—a tool designed by Griesbach and others to help us understand the Synoptic problem. Griesbach and Oxford proponents differ substantially; and the differences are enormous in implication. But they are united in this: the problem is worthy of study, and it makes a difference for interpretation, for history, for theology, and for pastoral theology.[55]

---

55. J. S. Kloppenborg, "The Theological Stakes in the Synoptic Problem," in *The Four Gospels—1992: Festschrift Frans Neirynck*, ed. F. van Segbroeck et al.; 3 vols., BETL 100 (Leuven: Leuven University Press), 1:93–120, provides an excellent example of how modern scholars sort out the differences that various solutions offer.

4

THE CASE FOR THE TWO-GOSPEL HYPOTHESIS

William R. Farmer

The genesis of this lecture can be traced back to my determination forty years ago to discover how it happened that I once stood before my students and assured them in good conscience that Mark was the earliest Gospel. It was not because of the arguments I then adduced in class. In fact, I distinctly recall feeling that there was a subtlety to the argument from order for Markan priority that I had never mastered. But the thought never crossed my mind that the argument itself was inconclusive. I used the argument without fully understanding it because it was an unquestioned part of an unquestioned tradition passed on to me by my teachers, whom I knew personally to be trustworthy and had good reasons to believe were professionally competent.

How had my teachers come to pass on to me the view that Mark was the earliest Gospel? This question led me back to investigate the history of the Synoptic problem. From one point of view, my book *The Synoptic Problem*[1] can be regarded as an act of *pietas*—a vindication of the integrity of my teachers—for it explained to me how they, like myself, could have done what they did in good conscience, and it also provided me the opportunity to demonstrate, by applying the high scholarly standards of critical inquiry they had taught me, the problematic character of the "critical consensus" all of us had inherited.

For anyone disposed to conclude that that book proves that the results of criticism are a snare and delusion, it need only be pointed out that criticism itself cannot be shown to be responsible for the "critical" consensus that developed by the early twentieth century that the priority of Mark and the existence of Q were two of the assured results of nineteenth-century biblical criticism. On the contrary, what is demonstrated in *The Synoptic Problem* is that consensus on some matters develops in spite of criticism and for reasons over which criticism has little control.

I spent the summer of 1962 preparing a polychrome *Synopticon*, which for the first time enabled me to grasp comprehensively verbatim agreement between the Gospels in all its totality.[2]

With this tool in hand, it was at last possible to proceed in a scientific manner to verify detailed points exhaustively, while at the same time viewing each detail in its widest possible context. The problem was then to consider the various ways in which the different phenomena of verbatim agreement between the Gospels could or could not be explained on alternate solutions of the problem. Finally, it was determined that one solution alone seemed to afford an explanation for all the phenomena. It then remained to isolate the phenomena that could be explained on that solution alone. This constituted evidence in favor of that solution and led to the formulation of arguments designed to communicate in examinable terms the significance of this evidence for the solution of the Synoptic problem. The next step was one of verification. This was carried out by a new literary analysis of the texts of Luke and Mark designed to test the cogency of the

1. William R. Farmer, *The Synoptic Problem: A Critical Analysis* (New York: Macmillan, 1964; repr. with corrections, Dillsboro, N.C.: Western North Carolina Press, 1976).
2. William R. Farmer, ed., *Synopticon: The Verbal Agreement between the Greek Texts of Matthew, Mark and Luke Contextually Exhibited* (Cambridge: Cambridge University Press, 1969).

arguments that had been formulated on the basis of the totality of the phenomena of verbatim agreement between the Gospels as abstracted through the aid of the *Synopticon*.

In making the case for the two-Gospel hypothesis in the year 2000, I begin by focusing attention on chapter 6 of *The Synoptic Problem*, composed over thirty-six years ago. In what follows I seek to bring up to date the case made in 1964 for the hypothesis that Luke copied Matthew, and Mark used both Matthew and Luke. In effect, this presentation is a modified and strengthened version of an argument that has stood the test of time and, in my opinion, warrants careful consideration even more today than ever before.

Before focusing on chapter 6, however, I draw upon a few pertinent comments made in the preface to *The Synoptic Problem*, in introducing this revised version.[3]

The Synoptic problem is difficult but not necessarily insoluble. Matthew, Mark, and Luke were almost certainly written in some particular chronological sequence. Reduced to its simplest terms, the Synoptic problem sets the task of discovering that compositional sequence. However important the part that oral tradition and other written sources may have played in the composition of the Synoptic Gospels, the problem of determining which was written first, which second, and which third persists. One of the three was written before the other two. One was written after the first and before the third. And one was written after the other two.

If a critic, on the basis of verified research, thinks that he or she knows the order in which Matthew, Mark, and Luke were written, and is asked to write about this question, there are alternative courses of action to consider: (1) One can attempt to write as if one did not know the truth, and strive to approach the problem with an objectivity that would reflect no particular point of view. In that case, to hypothecate a solution would require equally rigorous treatment of other possible solutions. The resulting study would be excessively burdensome, and therefore no such book has ever been written—the number of solutions that have been propounded is so great that the human

---

3. See William R. Farmer, *Selected Research Documents and Critical Essays in Support of the Two Gospel Hypothesis*, vol. 1, hereafter cited as *SRD*.

heart and hand falters before a task of such magnitude. (2) Another approach is to write about the problem from one's own point of view. In this case, the writer is obligated to disclose to readers the solution to the Synoptic problem being proposed, and to indicate something of the degree of probability that he or she attaches to it.

I follow the latter course in this essay. And the time has now come for the reader to know the point of view from which this essay has been written. Matthew appears to be the earliest Gospel, and Luke seems next in order. Matthew was evidently used extensively by the author of Luke, who also probably was the author of Acts. Luke undoubtedly had access to other written materials besides Matthew, and a very small portion of this material is parallel to material that Luke also found in Matthew. But Luke seems to be dependent on Matthew for the general order and form of his Gospel, and in many passages he appears clearly to have copied his text from Matthew.

There seems to be no sound literary or historical ground on which to base a denial of the premise that Mark throughout almost the whole extent of his Gospel appears to be working closely with texts of Matthew and Luke before him.

It is probable that there were other written sources and some kind of oral tradition also available to each of the evangelists. Matthew and Luke possibly had access to one or more common written sources. But the use of hypothetical written sources (and/or oral tradition) by the evangelists is not the best way to account for the major phenomena of similarity, including the extensive verbal agreement among Matthew, Mark, and Luke. This is best explained in terms of some direct literary relationship among all three.

Within this particular historical context, we find ourselves confronted with a view that calls into question a long-established consensus concerning one of the Gospels, namely, Mark. This view proposes for that Gospel a relationship to Matthew and Luke that is virtually the opposite of the relationship that it has on the consensus view. It will be helpful, therefore, if we make an effort to cut through the whole history of the problem and attempt to follow an argument intended to support the view that Luke was dependent on Matthew, and that Mark wrote after Matthew and Luke and is dependent upon both. This view is referred to today as the "two-gospel hypothesis."

Although the form and content of the particular argument set forth in chapter 6 of my 1964 book drew upon much that had been done previously, at the time of writing it was to a large extent new. That 1964 argument was intended to encourage a serious reconsideration of a solution first formulated in the eighteenth century, which flourished in the first half of the nineteenth century, but which during the intervening one hundred years had been eclipsed by the two-source hypothesis, that Mark was the earliest Gospel and that the later Gospels Matthew and Luke made use of Mark and a hypothetical source called Q.

The argument for Mark being dependent on both Matthew and Luke was presented in steps. At first it is important for the reader to take one step at a time and always in order. But as one advances through the initial steps, it matters little in what order one takes the later steps, some of which indeed may be skipped without decisive loss. That is, the cogency of the argument does not presuppose that the separable theses presented at each step in the argument are like the links of a chain, which, as a chain, can be no stronger than the weakest link. On the contrary, the cogency of this argument depends upon a web of evidence structured by innumerable arguments, some of which touch only the most minute points, but which, nevertheless, taken together with all the rest, constitute a supportive basis that will bear the weight of the conclusion: it is historically probable that Mark was written after Matthew and Luke and was dependent upon both. The destruction of one or more of the strands of evidence that have been woven into this web would not destroy the web.

In 1964 it was acknowledged that subsequent research might damage the web so that it could no longer hold up the conclusion it was spun to support. What has actually happened since 1964, however, is that no research has been published and verified that results in the destruction of a single strand in this web of argumentation. In fact, quite the opposite has happened. While recognized experts have criticized one or two strands in this argument, these criticisms have all been carefully answered in the scientific literature.

In 1964 it was also acknowledged that other critics might see ways in which the web of evidence could be strengthened by adding an argument here and by restructuring another one there. David L. Dungan was the first critic to do this, with his essay "Mark: The Abridgment of Matthew and Luke"[4] (see SRD, vol. 1.). Since that time, one after another, a series of critics, through their research, have added strength to this web of argumentation, until today it is generally acknowledged (at least on this side of the Atlantic) that the hypothesis that Luke used Matthew and that Mark was composed after Matthew and Luke is at present the best-defended critical alternative to the still widely utilized two-source hypothesis.

Step 1

Thesis: *The similarity between Matthew, Mark, and Luke is such as to justify the assertion that they stand in some kind of literary relationship to one another.*

The nature of this similarity is such as to warrant the judgment that the literary relationship between these Gospels could be one involving direct copying. That is, the degree of verbatim agreement in Greek between any two of these three Gospels is as high or higher than that which generally exists between documents where it is known that the author of one copied the text of the other. The same degree of verbatim agreement could be accounted for on the hypothesis that each evangelist independently copied one or more common or genetically related sources. But this alternative way of explaining the phenomena of agreement between any two Gospels should not be utilized until after an attempt has been made to explain it on the simplest terms, namely, on the hypothesis that one evangelist copied the work of the other. The reason for this procedure is not that the simplest explanation is necessarily the correct one, but that it is methodologically wrong to multiply hypothetical possibilities *unnecessarily.* There is nothing wrong in hypothecating the existence of an otherwise unknown source or sources, if there exists evidence that is best explained thereby; but, for the sake of economy this is not to be done without good reason. This is not an infallible rule, but it is accepted procedure in liter-

4. In *Jesus and Man's Hope,* 2 vols. (Pittsburgh: Pittsburgh Theological Seminary, 1970), 1:51–97.

ary criticism as well as in other disciplines, and one that commends itself by the results achieved when it is followed, compared to those achieved when it is ignored.

The following specimens of texts of Matthew, Mark, and Luke are presented as illustrations of the kind of verbal similarity that exists among these Gospels, and suggests the possibility of direct copying.

Every word underlined is found in the parallel text(s) of the other Gospel(s) printed on the same page. If the underlining is unbroken, the agreement is exact with reference to case, declension, number, and gender of nouns, articles, pronouns, adjectives, and participles; and exact with reference to mood, voice, tense, number, and person of verbs. Broken underlining indicates agreement as to the word concerned, but where the agreement is not exact in one or more points of grammar. Differences in the endings of words merely occasioned by the circumstance of their position in the sentence, like the movable *nu*, or by the circumstance of the quality of the initial letter of the word following, as with the ending of the negative οὐ, are disregarded. A continuation of underlining between words indicates that the same words not only occur in the other Gospel(s) printed on the same page, but also that they occur in exactly the same order.

The Feeding of the Four Thousand

(Not in Luke.)

Matthew 15:32–39

Ὁ δὲ Ἰησοῦς προσκαλεσάμενος τοὺς μαθητὰς αὐτοῦ εἶπεν· σπλαγχνίζομαι ἐπὶ τὸν ὄχλον, ὅτι ἤδη ἡμέραι τρεῖς προσμένουσίν μοι καὶ οὐκ ἔχουσιν τί φάγωσιν· καὶ ἀπολῦσαι αὐτοὺς νήστεις οὐ θέλω, μήποτε ἐκλυθῶσιν ἐν τῇ ὁδῷ· καὶ λέγουσιν αὐτῷ οἱ μαθηταί· πόθεν ἡμῖν ἐν ἐρημίᾳ ἄρτοι τοσοῦτοι ὥστε χορτάσαι ὄχλον τοσοῦτον; καὶ λέγει αὐτοῖς ὁ Ἰησοῦς· πόσους ἄρτους ἔχετε; οἱ δὲ εἶπαν· ἑπτά καὶ ὀλίγα ἰχθύδια. καὶ παραγγείλας τῷ ὄχλῳ ἀναπεσεῖν ἐπὶ τὴν γῆν ἔλαβεν τοὺς ἑπτὰ ἄρτους καὶ τοὺς ἰχθύας καὶ εὐχαριστήσας ἔκλασεν καὶ ἐδίδου τοῖς μαθηταῖς, οἱ δὲ μαθηταὶ τοῖς ὄχλοις. καὶ ἔφαγον πάντες καὶ ἐχορτάσθησαν, καὶ τὸ περισσεῦον τῶν κλασμάτων ἦραν ἑπτὰ σπυρίδας πλήρεις. οἱ δὲ ἐσθίοντες ἦσαν τετρακισχίλιοι ἄνδρες χωρὶς γυναικῶν καὶ παιδίων. καὶ ἀπολύσας τοὺς ὄχλους ἐνέβη εἰς τὸ πλοῖον καὶ ἦλθεν εἰς τὰ ὅρια Μαγαδάν.

Mark 8:1–10

Ἐν ἐκείναις ταῖς ἡμέραις πάλιν πολλοῦ ὄχλου ὄντος καὶ μὴ ἐχόντων τί φάγωσιν, προσκαλεσάμενος τοὺς μαθητὰς λέγει αὐτοῖς· σπλαγχνίζομαι ἐπὶ τὸν ὄχλον, ὅτι ἤδη ἡμέραι τρεῖς προσμένουσίν μοι καὶ οὐκ ἔχουσιν τί φάγωσιν· καὶ ἐὰν ἀπολύσω αὐτοὺς νήστεις εἰς οἶκον αὐτῶν, ἐκλυθήσονται ἐν τῇ ὁδῷ· καί τινες αὐτῶν ἀπὸ μακρόθεν ἥκασιν. καὶ ἀπεκρίθησαν αὐτῷ οἱ μαθηταὶ αὐτοῦ ὅτι πόθεν τούτους δυνήσεταί τις ὧδε χορτάσαι ἄρτων ἐπ᾽ ἐρημίας; καὶ ἠρώτα αὐτούς· πόσους ἔχετε ἄρτους; οἱ δὲ εἶπαν· ἑπτά. καὶ παραγγέλλει τῷ ὄχλῳ ἀναπεσεῖν ἐπὶ τῆς γῆς· καὶ λαβὼν τοὺς ἑπτὰ ἄρτους εὐχαριστήσας ἔκλασεν καὶ ἐδίδου τοῖς μαθηταῖς αὐτοῦ ἵνα παρατιθῶσιν, καὶ παρέθηκαν τῷ ὄχλῳ, καὶ εἶχον ἰχθύδια ὀλίγα· καὶ εὐλογήσας αὐτὰ εἶπεν καὶ ταῦτα παρατιθέναι. καὶ ἔφαγον καὶ ἐχορτάσθησαν, καὶ ἦραν περισσεύματα κλασμάτων ἑπτὰ σπυρίδας. ἦσαν δὲ ὡς τετρακισχίλιοι.

Often, the agreement between Matthew and Mark is more extensive than in this passage, though many times it is less so. This passage, however, is not atypical. See Matt. 26:20–29 // Mark 14:17–25; Matt. 26:36–46 // Mark 14:32–42 as examples where the verbatim agreement between Matthew and Mark is greater than in the specimens cited.

Jesus in the Synagogue at Capernaum

(Not in Matthew.)

Mark 1:21–28

Καὶ εἰσπορεύονται εἰς Καφαρναούμ. καὶ εὐθὺς τοῖς σάββασιν εἰσελθὼν εἰς τὴν συναγωγὴν ἐδίδασκεν. καὶ ἐξεπλήσσοντο ἐπὶ τῇ διδαχῇ αὐτοῦ· ἦν γὰρ διδάσκων αὐτοὺς ὡς ἐξουσίαν ἔχων καὶ οὐχ ὡς οἱ γραμματεῖς. καὶ εὐθὺς ἦν ἐν τῇ συναγωγῇ αὐτῶν ἄνθρωπος ἐν πνεύματι ἀκαθάρτῳ, καὶ ἀνέκραξεν λέγων· τί ἡμῖν καὶ σοί, Ἰησοῦ Ναζαρηνέ; ἦλθες ἀπολέσαι ἡμᾶς; οἶδά σε τίς εἶ, ὁ ἅγιος τοῦ θεοῦ. καὶ ἐπετίμησεν αὐτῷ ὁ Ἰησοῦς λέγων· φιμώθητι καὶ ἔξελθε ἐξ

αὐτοῦ. καὶ σπαράξαν αὐτὸν τὸ πνεῦμα τὸ ἀκάθαρτον καὶ φω-
νῆσαν φωνῇ μεγάλῃ ἐξῆλθεν ἐξ αὐτοῦ. καὶ ἐθαμβήθησαν ἅπαντες
ὥστε συζητεῖν πρὸς ἑαυτοὺς λέγοντας· τί ἐστιν τοῦτο; διδαχὴ
καινὴ κατ᾽ ἐξουσίαν· καὶ τοῖς πνεύμασι τοῖς ἀκαθάρτοις ἐπιτάσσει, καὶ ὑπακούουσιν αὐτῷ. καὶ ἐξῆλθεν ἡ ἀκοὴ αὐτοῦ εὐθὺς
πανταχοῦ εἰς ὅλην τὴν περίχωρον τῆς Γαλιλαίας.

Luke 4:31–37

Καὶ κατῆλθεν εἰς Καφαρναοὺμ πόλιν τῆς Γαλιλαίας. καὶ ἦν
διδάσκων αὐτοὺς ἐν τοῖς σαββασιν· καὶ ἐξεπλήσσοντο ἐπὶ τῇ διδαχῇ αὐτοῦ, ὅτι ἐν ἐξουσίᾳ ἦν ὁ λόγος αὐτοῦ. καὶ ἐν τῇ συναγωγῇ
ἦν ἄνθρωπος ἔχων πνεῦμα δαιμονίου ἀκαθάρτου καὶ ἀνέκραξεν
φωνῇ μεγάλῃ· ἔα, τί ἡμῖν καὶ σοί, Ἰησοῦ Ναζαρηνέ; ἦλθες ἀπολέσαι ἡμᾶς; οἶδά σε τίς εἶ, ὁ ἅγιος τοῦ θεοῦ. καὶ ἐπετίμησεν αὐτῷ ὁ
Ἰησοῦς λέγων· φιμώθητι καὶ ἔξελθε ἀπ᾽ αὐτοῦ. καὶ ῥῖψαν αὐτὸν τὸ
δαιμόνιον εἰς τὸ μέσον ἐξῆλθεν ἀπ᾽ αὐτοῦ μηδὲν βλάψαν αὐτόν.
καὶ ἐγένετο θάμβος ἐπὶ πάντας, καὶ συνελάλουν πρὸς ἀλλήλους
λέγοντες· τίς ὁ λόγος οὗτος, ὅτι ἐν ἐξουσίᾳ καὶ δυνάμει ἐπιτάσσει
τοῖς ἀκαθάρτοις πνεύμασιν καὶ ἐξέρχονται; καὶ ἐξεπορεύετο ἦχος
περὶ αὐτοῦ εἰς πάντα τόπον τῆς περιχώρου.

The verbatim agreement between Mark and Luke is not as extensive as between Mark and Matthew. But the reader can
readily see from this specimen and a comparison of the following examples that the verbal similarity between Mark and Luke
is quite extensive: Mark 5:1–20 // Luke 8:26–39; Mark 9:37–40 //
Luke 9:48–50; Mark 10:17–31 // Luke 18:18–30; Mark 12:38b–44
// Luke 20:46–21:4.

The Centurion's Servant

(Not in Mark.)

Matthew 8:7–10

καὶ λέγει αὐτῷ· ἐγὼ ἐλθὼν θεραπεύσω αὐτόν. καὶ ἀποκριθεὶς δὲ
ὁ ἑκατόνταρχος ἔφη· κύριε, οὐκ εἰμὶ ἱκανὸς ἵνα μου ὑπὸ τὴν στέγην
εἰσέλθῃς, ἀλλὰ μόνον εἰπὲ λόγῳ, καὶ ἰαθήσεται ὁ παῖς μου. καὶ γὰρ
ἐγὼ ἄνθρωπός εἰμι ὑπὸ ἐξουσίαν, ἔχων ὑπ᾽ ἐμαυτὸν στρατιώτας,
καὶ λέγω τούτῳ· πορεύθητι, καὶ πορεύεται, καὶ ἄλλῳ· ἔρχου, καὶ

ἔρχεται, καὶ τῷ δούλῳ μου· ποίησον τοῦτο, καὶ ποιεῖ. ἀκούσας δὲ ὁ Ἰησοῦς ἐθαύμασεν καὶ εἶπεν τοῖς ἀκολουθοῦσιν· ἀμὴν λέγω ὑμῖν, παρ᾽ οὐδενὶ τοσαύτην πίστιν ἐν τῷ Ἰσραὴλ εὗπον.

Luke 7:6–9

ὁ δὲ Ἰησοῦς ἐπορεύετο σὺν αὐτοῖς. ἤδη δὲ αὐτοῦ οὐ μακρὰν ἀπέχοντος ἀπὸ τῆς οἰκίας ἔπεμψεν φίλους ὁ ἑκατοντάρχης λέγων αὐτῷ· κύριε, μὴ σκύλλου, οὐ γὰρ ἱκανός εἰμι ἵνα ὑπὸ τὴν στέγην μου εἰσέλθῃς· διὸ οὐδὲ ἐμαυτὸν ἠξίωσα πρὸς σὲ ἐλθεῖν· ἀλλὰ εἰπὲ λόγῳ, καὶ ἰαθήτω ὁ παῖς μου. καὶ γὰρ ἐγὼ ἄνθρωπός εἰμι ὑπὸ ἐξουσίαν τασσόμενος ἔχων ὑπ᾽ ἐμαυτὸν στρατιώτας, καὶ λέγω τούτῳ· πορεύθητι, καὶ πορεύεται, καὶ ἄλλῳ· ἔρχου, καὶ ἔρχεται, καὶ τῷ δούλῳ μου· ποίησον τοῦτο, καὶ ποιεῖ. ἀκούσας δὲ ταῦτα ὁ Ἰησοῦς ἐθαύμασεν αὐτόν καὶ στραφεὶς τῷ ἀκολουθοῦντι αὐτῷ ὄχλῳ εἶπεν· λέγω ὑμῖν οὐδὲ ἐν τῷ Ἰσραὴλ τοσαύτην πίστιν εὗρον.

The verbatim agreement between Luke and Matthew in this passage is equaled or exceeded at many points. See, for example, Luke 3:7–9 // Matt. 3:7–10; Luke 4:1–13 // Matt. 4:1–11; Luke 6:41–42 // Matt. 7:3–5; Luke 7:18–35 // Matt. 11:2–19; Luke 11:29–32 // Matt. 12:38–42; Luke 13:34–35 // Matt. 23:37–39.

Not only is there extensive agreement between any two of the Synoptic Gospels, but also there are many passages characterized by extensive agreement among all three. See, for example, Matt. 8:2–4 // Mark 1:40–45 // Luke 5:12–16.

The Healing of a Leper

Matthew 8:2–4

καὶ ἰδοὺ λεπρὸς προσελθὼν προσεκύνει αὐτῷ λέγων· κύριε, ἐὰν θέλῃς δύνασαί με καθαρίσαι. καὶ ἐκτείνας τὴν χεῖρα ἥψατο αὐτοῦ λέγων· θέλω, καθαρίσθητι· καὶ εὐθέως ἐκαθαρίσθη αὐτοῦ ἡ λέπρα. καὶ λέγει αὐτῷ ὁ Ἰησοῦς· ὅρα μηδενὶ εἴπῃς, ἀλλὰ ὕπαγε σεαυτὸν δεῖξον τῷ ἱερεῖ καὶ προσένεγκον τὸ δῶρον ὃ προσέταξεν Μωϋσῆς, εἰς μαρτύριον αὐτοῖς.

Mark 1:40–45

Καὶ ἔρχεται πρὸς αὐτὸν λεπρὸς παρακαλῶν αὐτὸν καὶ γονυ-
πετῶν καὶ λέγων αὐτῷ ὅτι ἐὰν θέλῃς δύνασαί με καθαρίσαι.
καὶ σπαγχνισθεὶς ἐκτείας τὴν χεῖρα αὐτοῦ ἥψατο καὶ λέγει αὐτῷ·
θέλω, καθαρίσθητι· καὶ εὐθὺς ἀπῆλθεν ἀπ᾽ αὐτοῦ ἡ λέπρα, καὶ
ἐκαθαρίσθη. καὶ ἐμβριμησάμενος αὐτῷ εὐθὺς ἐξέβαλεν αὐτὸν καὶ
λέγει αὐτῷ· ὅρα μηδενὶ μηδὲν εἴπῃς, ἀλλὰ ὕπαγε σεαυτὸν δεῖξον τῷ
ἱερεῖ καὶ προσένεγκε περὶ τοῦ καθαρισμοῦ σου ἃ προσέταξεν
Μωϋσῆς, εἰς μαρτύριον αὐτοῖς. ὁ δὲ ἐξελθὼν ἤρξατο κηρύσσειν
πολλὰ καὶ διαφημίζειν τὸν λόγον, ὥστε μηκέτι αὐτὸν δύνασθαι
φανερῶς εἰς πόλιν εἰσελθεῖν, ἀλλ᾽ ἔξω ἐπ᾽ ἐρήμοις τόποις ἦν· καὶ
ἤρχοντο πρὸς αὐτὸν πάντοθεν.

Luke 5:12–16

Καὶ ἐγένετο ἐν τῷ εἶναι αὐτὸν ἐν μιᾷ τῶν πόλεων καὶ ἰδοὺ ἀνὴρ
πλήρης λέπρας· ἰδὼν δὲ τὸν Ἰησοῦν, πεσὼν ἐπὶ πρόσωπον ἐδεήθη αὐτοῦ λέγων· κύριε, ἐὰν θέλῃς, δύνασαί με καθαρίσαι. καὶ ἐκτείνας τὴν
χεῖρα ἥψατο αὐτοῦ λέγων· θέλω, καθαρίσθητι· καὶ εὐθέως ἡ λέπρα
ἀπῆλθεν ἀπ᾽ αὐτοῦ. καὶ αὐτὸς παρήγγειλεν αὐτῷ μηδενὶ εἰπεῖν, ἀλλὰ
ἀπελθὼν δεῖξον σεαυτὸν τῷ ἱερεῖ καὶ προσένεγκε περὶ τοῦ καθαρισμοῦ σου καθὼς προσέταξεν Μωϋσῆς, εἰς μαρτύριον αὐτοῖς. διήρ-
χετο δὲ μᾶλλον ὁ λόγος περὶ αὐτοῦ, καὶ συνήρχοντο ὄχλοι πολλοὶ
ἀκούειν καὶ θεραπεύεσθαι ἀπὸ τῶν ἀσθενειῶν αὐτῶν· αὐτὸς δὲ ἦν
ὑποχωρῶν ἐν ταῖς ἐρήμοις καὶ προσευχόμενος.

Among the other passages that exhibit extensive agreement
among all three Synoptics, the following may be considered as
more or less representative:

Matt. 9:1–8 // Mark 2:1–12 // Luke 5:17–26
Matt. 16:24–28 // Mark 8:34–9:1 // Luke 9:23–27
Matt. 19:13–15 // Mark 10:13–16 // Luke 18:15–17
Matt. 21:23–27 // Mark 11:27–33 // Luke 20:1–8
Matt. 21:33–46 // Mark 12:1–12 // Luke 20:9–19
Matt. 22:23–33 // Mark 12:18–27 // Luke 20:27–40
Matt. 24:4–8 // Mark 13:5–8 // Luke 21:8–11

Step 2

Thesis: *There are eighteen, and only eighteen, fundamental ways in which three documents among which there exists some kind of direct literary dependence may be related to one another.*

If the second copied the first, and the third copied the second but not the first, they may be related to one another thus in six different ways:

If the first and second were independent of one another, and the third copied both predecessors, they may be related to one another thus in three different ways:

If the second and third independently copied the first, they may be related to one another thus in three different ways:

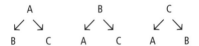

If the second copied the first, and the third copied both predecessors, they may be related to one another thus in six different ways:

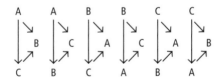

Step 3

Thesis: *While it is possible to conceive of an infinite number of variations of these eighteen basic relationships by positing additional hypothetical documents, these eighteen should be given first consideration.*

The reasons for this have been indicated in the discussion of step 1. This does not mean that the investigator should assume that there were no additional hypothetical documents. On the contrary, the possibility that such documents actually existed should be left open. There are instances in literary-historical studies where circumstantial evidence requires the investigator to posit the existence of a document for which there is no direct evidence. But a critic should not posit the existence of hypothetical documents without first having made an attempt to solve the problem without appeal to hypothetical documents. Only after the investigator has been unable to understand the relationship between Matthew, Mark, and Luke without appealing to unknown sources is there justification in hypothecating the existence of such sources, in order to explain phenomena otherwise inexplicable.

Step 4

Thesis: *Only six out of eighteen basic hypothetical arrangements are viable.*

This follows from the circumstances that there are agreements between any two of the Synoptic Gospels against the third.

This is a verifiable point, recognized by all careful investigators, and it provides an important clue to the solution of the problem once it is properly understood. For if one does not begin by appealing to hypothetical documents, but rather concentrates attention on the eighteen basic arrangements set forth in step 2, it follows that where any two Gospels agree, and the third does not (either because the third has something different or is silent), that of the two Gospels between which verbal agreement exists, the Gospel written earlier was copied by the author of the Gospel written later. Without hypothecating a nonexistent document (like Q), the agreement could not otherwise be explained.

But if there are agreements between Matthew and Mark against Luke, and Matthew and Luke against Mark, and Luke and Mark against Matthew, then no one of these eighteen basic hypotheses is valid that fails to provide for some kind of a direct literary dependence among all three.

Thus, all six instances where the second evangelist copied the work of the first, and the third copied the second but not the first, can be eliminated from further consideration. For under such circumstances it would be impossible for the first and third to agree with one another against the second.

The three instances where the first and the second are independent of one another and the third copied both may also be eliminated from further consideration. For under such circumstances it would be impossible for the first and the second to agree with one another against the third.

Similarly, the three cases where the second and third independently copied the first may be eliminated from consideration. For on this proposed solution there is no known way (short of hypothecating an unknown common source written in Greek) to explain how the second and third could agree against the first.

But in those six cases where the second writer copied the first, and the third had direct access to both the first and the second, the situation is quite different. For these six cases do afford the opportunity for any two of the Synoptic Gospels to agree against the third. Thus, for example, agreements between the first and the second against the third would result from circumstances where the second copied something from the first that the third did not copy exactly or at all, either from the first or the second. And agreements between the second and the third against the first would result from circumstances where the third copied something from the second which was not in the first. And finally, agreements between the first and the third against the second would result from circumstances where the third copied something from the first that the second had copied less exactly or not at all.

It follows from the above that whichever evangelist was third faced the problem of working with two Gospels between which there already existed a relation of direct literary dependence, in that the second had copied the first. There are certain definite redactional limitations and possibilities within which a writer under such circumstances is able to function, and this provides us a clue for discerning which of the evangelists was in the position of being third. A writer in the position of being third can (1) follow the text to which both earlier Gospels bear concurrent testimony; (2) deviate from one, but follow the other, when his sources disagree; (3) attempt to combine them where they disagree; (4) deviate by omission or alteration from both when they disagree; (5) deviate by omission or alteration from both even when they do agree.

Is it possible to isolate and objectively define categories of literary phenomena that are more readily explicable when one of the evangelists is placed third than when either of the other two is placed third? The answer is yes.

Step 5

Thesis: *There are isolatable and objectively definable categories of literary phenomena that play a prominent role in the history of the Synoptic problem that when properly understood are more readily explicable when Mark is placed third than when either Matthew or Luke is placed third.*

These are two in number: (1) the phenomena of order and content; (2) the so-called minor agreements of Matthew and Luke against Mark. (See *SRD*, vol. 4.)

There is a third literary phenomenon that has seldom been noted, but is also more readily explicable when Mark is third than in any other position. This is the otherwise inexplicable positive correlation of order and degree of similarity between Matthew and Mark on the one hand and Luke and Mark on the other. That is, Mark tends to agree more closely with Matthew when these two evangelists follow an order different from Luke, but more closely with Luke when they follow an order different from Matthew.

Step 6

Thesis: *The phenomena of agreement and disagreement in the respective order and content of material in each of the Synoptic Gospels constitute a category of literary phenomena that is more readily explicable on a hypothesis that places Mark third with Matthew and Luke before him than on any alternative hypothesis.*

With very few exceptions, which are no more difficult for one hypothesis than for any other, the order of material in Mark never departs from the order of material common to Matthew and Luke. Therefore, Matthew and Luke almost never agree in order against Mark. If Mark was third, this fact would be readily explained by the reasonable assumption that the evangelist writing third had little or no chronological information apart from that which he found in Matthew and Luke, or that if he did, he preferred not to interrupt the order of events common to these two Gospels.

When the order of Matthew and Luke is not the same, the order of Mark tends to be the same as either the one or the other. If Mark was third, this fact would be readily explained by the same assumption stated above, and the recognition that when Mark was confronted by a situation where his sources departed from one another in order, so that there was no longer a common order to follow, he tended to follow the order of one or the other of his sources rather than depart from both. This cannot be imagined as an unnatural procedure for Mark to have followed under such circumstances. A similar statement can be made concerning the content of Mark. Mark seldom has a story or a saying that is not found either in Matthew or Luke or both. The major exceptions to this statement are two healing stories (Mark 7:32–35; 8:22–26) and one parable (Mark 4:26–29).

On the two-Gospel hypothesis this is readily explained either by the circumstances that Mark was in fact limited to drawing material for his Gospel primarily from Matthew and Luke, or that he chose to limit himself to these sources.[5]

Confining the possibilities to the six viable hypotheses set forth in step 4, it is possible to say that only the two hypotheses that place Mark third afford a ready explanation for the phenomenon of agreement in order and content among Matthew, Mark, and Luke. Thus:

---

5. In the original version of step 6 there follows at this point a demonstration eliminating four of the six viable hypothetical arrangements listed at the end of step 2.

The choice between these two hypotheses cannot be made on the basis of order and content, but must be settled on other grounds.

Step 7

Thesis: *The minor agreements of Matthew and Luke against Mark constitute a second category of literary phenomena that is more readily explicable on a hypothesis where Mark is regarded as third with Matthew and Luke before him than on any alternative hypothesis.*

In a typical passage where all three Gospels have parallel material there tend to be seven distinguishable categories of literary phenomena: (1) agreements among all three; (2) agreements between Matthew and Mark against Luke; (3) agreements between Mark and Luke against Matthew; (4) agreements between Matthew and Luke against Mark; (5) words unique to Matthew; (6) words unique to Mark; and (7) words unique to Luke.

Categories 2, 3, and 4 are manifestly distinguishable from 1, 5, 6, and 7. When categories 2, 3, and 4 are compared, it is found that 4 is distinguishable from 2 and 3, in that the agreements in 2 and 3 tend to be more extensive and substantial than those in 4. That is, in passages where all three Gospels are parallel, the agreements between Matthew and Luke against Mark more often than not are minor in extent, inconsequential in substance, and sporadic in occurrence, as compared to the corresponding phenomena in categories 2 and 3. This is not true without exception. But it is true in the great majority of cases, and it requires some explanation. There is no ready explanation for this phenomenon, except on the hypothesis that Luke frequently followed the text of Matthew clearly, and that Mark, being third, chose to follow closely the text(s) of his predecessors whenever Luke had followed very closely the text of Matthew. The reason for Mark to follow such a compositional procedure flows naturally from his authorial intent to produce a text that would be in essential agreement with the texts of his predecessors whenever they were in close agreement. (For detailed evidence concerning alleged agreements between Matthew and Luke in omitting details from the text of Mark, see *SRD*, vol. 4.) The simplest explanation for these alleged omissions is to regard them as due to Mark's being third and exercising his authorial freedom to add details to the text he is composing, while drawing his material largely from Matthew and Luke.

Step 8

Thesis: *There exists a positive correlation between agreement in order and agreement in wording among the Synoptic Gospels that is most readily explicable on the hypothesis that Mark was written after Matthew and Luke and is the result of a redactional procedure in which Mark made use both of Matthew and Luke.*

When Matthew, Mark, and Luke do not all three agree in order, as has been pointed out, either Matthew and Mark will agree in order or Luke and Mark will agree in order. The point is that when Matthew and Mark are following the same order, but Luke exhibits a different order, the texts of Matthew and Mark tend to be closer to one another. And when Luke and Mark are following the same order, but Matthew exhibits a different order, the texts of Luke and Mark tend to be closer to one another. This is quite noticeable in the first half of Mark, and requires an explanation.

This phenomenon is especially difficult to explain on any hypothesis that presupposes that Matthew and Luke independently copied Mark or *Urmarcus*. For, since Matthew had no knowledge of Luke's redactional use of Mark, there is no way he could have known to begin copying the text of Mark more closely where Luke's order was different from that of Mark. Conversely, there is no way in which Luke could have known to begin copying the text of Mark more closely at the point where Mark's order and that of Matthew departed from one another.

On the two-Gospel hypothesis, however, there is a ready explanation for the whole of this phenomenon. For it would not have been unnatural for Mark to have given some preference to the text of Matthew when he had deliberately chosen to follow Matthew's order instead of that of Luke, and conversely, it would not have been unnatural for him to have given some preference to the text of Luke when he had deliberately chosen to follow Luke's order in preference to that of Matthew. One would not expect Mark to follow such a procedure inflexibly. Indeed, the phenomenon is ambiguous enough to indicate that if in fact Mark was third, he did not follow this pattern with absolute consistency. Nevertheless, a positive correlation does exist, which was recognized by the nineteenth-century advocates of the Griesbach hypothesis. "When the same facts, which are recorded by the evangelist whom he [Mark] is following at any time, are narrated also by the other, he makes use of the latter also, to guide him in his manner of description, and even of expression, but he keeps mainly to the former."[6] Assuming Mark to be third and working with Matthew and Luke, this statement does justice to a particular literary phenomenon of the Gospels themselves. The point is that it does not seem possible on any other hypothesis to make a similar statement that will take into account the same phenomenon equally as well.[7]

Step 9

Thesis: *It is possible to understand the compositional process followed in producing the Gospel according to Mark based on the hypothesis that the author drew primarily on the texts of Matthew and Luke.*

A demonstration of this thesis is given in chapter 7 of *The Synoptic Problem*. The reader is further referred to the nineteenth-century works of de Wette and Bleek.[8] A thorough and

6. Friedrich Bleek, *An Introduction to the New Testament*, trans. W. Urwick, 2 vols., 2nd ed. (Edinburgh: T. & T. Clark, 1869–70), 1:267.

7. The reader is referred to chapter 7 of Farmer, *Synoptic Problem*, for the specific confirmation of this thesis (see *SRD*, vol. 1). It is very important not to think that this correlation can be easily verified. There are places where no correlation seems apparent. But there is generally an understandable reason for the fact that in some places the matter is ambiguous, which is readily forthcoming on the two-Gospel hypothesis.

8. See especially Wilhelm Martin Leberecht De Wette, "Erklärung des Verhältnisses zwischen Marcus und den beiden andern Evangelisten durch die Annahme, dass er sie benutz hat," in *Lehrbuch der historisch-kritischen Einleitung in die kanonischen Bücher des Neuen Testaments*, 5th ed., 167–79; idem, "Evangelium des Marcus," in *Kurze Erklärung der Evangelien des Lukas und Markus*, Kurzgefaßtes exegetisches Handbuch zum Neuen Testament 1.2 (Leipzig: Weidmann'sche, 1839), 127–200. See also paragraphs 93–97 in Friedrich Bleek, *Einleitung in das Neue Testament*, 2nd ed. (Berlin: Reimer,

comprehensive pericope by pericope demonstration of how, on the two-Gospel hypothesis, Mark made use of Matthew and Luke is near completion and scheduled for publication in 2001. A new electronic synopsis of Mark will accompany the Trinity Press International publication of this book. This book on Mark is being authored by the same research team that produced *Beyond the Q Impasse*, and will be edited by David B. Peabody, author of *Mark as Composer*.[9] The electronic synopsis of Mark has been created by Peabody and Thomas Longstaff. Longstaff is the author of *Evidence of Conflation in Mark? A Study in the Synoptic Problem*.[10]

Step 10

Thesis: *The most probable explanation for the extensive agreement between Matthew and Luke is that the author of one made use of the work of the other.*

Such a direct literary dependence between Matthew and Luke is not incompatible with their mutual use of common sources. Where each has material that is similar, but where there is insufficient evidence to warrant the judgment that there was direct copying by one evangelist of the work of the other—for example, as is the case in one or two parables—the explanation that a common source has been copied is altogether plausible. But where the evidence for direct literary dependence is strong, as it is in the so-called Q material, the most probable explanation would be that one of the evangelists copied the work of the other.

The hypothesis that either the author of Matthew or the author of Luke had the work of the other before him affords a ready explanation not only for the extensive agreement in con-

---

1866). (In the English translation, Bleek, *Introduction to the New Testament,* this section is set forth under the heading "Dependence of Mark upon Matthew and Luke," 1:258–75). See also Samuel Davidson, "The Gospel of Mark—'Analysis of Contents,' and 'Relation of Mark to Matthew and Luke,'" in *An Introduction to the Study of the New Testament, Critical, Exegetical, and Theological,* 2 vols., 2nd ed. (London: Kegan Paul, Trench, Trübner, 1882), 1:542–63.

9. A. J. McNicol, ed., with D. L. Dungan and D. B. Peabody, *Beyond the Q Impasse* (Valley Forge, Pa.: Trinity Press International, 1996); David B. Peabody, *Mark as Composer,* NGS 1 (Macon, Ga.: Mercer University Press, 1987).

10. SBLDS 28 (Missoula, Mont.: Scholars, 1977).

tent between the works of these two evangelists, but also for their remarkable similarities in literary form.

Both Matthew and Luke begin with birth narratives, contain genealogies, begin Jesus' ministry with his baptism by John, record the teachings of John, picture Jesus tempted by Satan in the wilderness, describe Jesus' ministry in Galilee, introduce into their narrative framework large collections of Jewish gnomic and parabolic materials (including primitive sayings reflecting the historical solidarity between Jesus and John), and narrate Jesus' journey to Jerusalem with his disciples, his triumphal entry, his cleansing of the temple, the Last Supper with his disciples, the arrest in Gethsemane, the trial before the high priest and before Pilate, and finally, the crucifixion, death, burial, and resurrection of Jesus.

The fact that in some parts of this outline Luke introduced different content indicates only that he had ample reason to write a new Gospel, and in no way explains why he follows a literary scheme so similar to that found in Matthew. When compared to other Gospel literature in particular, and to contemporary Hellenistic and Jewish literature in general, Matthew and Luke bear a striking resemblance to one another both in form and content.

The form of Matthew and Luke is unique in literature. It is unlikely that two writers would independently have created such unique and at the same time such similar literary works. It is altogether probable that one was the prototype of the other, that one was the original literary creation, and that the author of the other took this original work as his literary exemplar, making such improvements and modifications as may have been in line with his known literary and theological purposes.[11]

It is not possible to explain the similarity in content and form between Matthew and Luke by positing their mutual dependence upon either John or Mark without making appeal to one or more additional sources, all hypothetical, to explain material held in common by Matthew and Luke not found in either John or Mark. Therefore, as long as one seeks to solve the Synoptic problem without having recourse to conjectural sources like Q, one is led to posit direct literary dependence between Luke and Matthew.

11. See Bernard Orchard, *Matthew, Luke and Mark* (Manchester: Koinonia, 1976).

Step 11

Thesis: *The hypothesis that Luke made use of Matthew is in accord with Luke's statement in the prologue to his Gospel concerning his purpose in writing.*

The usual interpretation of Luke 1:1, that at the time Luke wrote there were many Gospels in existence, is linguistically possible though not necessary. Lessing interpreted Luke as meaning that "many have undertaken to rearrange a narrative," and concluded that this referred to an original narrative, composed by the apostles, which Lessing identified with "the Gospel of the Nazarenes."[12] The important point linguistically is that the word διήγησιν is singular. Therefore, it would be possible to understand Luke to have referred to a single narrative, which he did not think of as the work of a single individual, but of πολλοί. For it is not necessary to translate ἀνατάξασθαι as "rearrange." The Greek can be rendered "many have undertaken to *compile* a narrative."

This was a possible way for Luke to have viewed the Gospel of Matthew. For while it is not impossible that a single individual played an important part in the final stage in the redaction of all the tradition that was included in Matthew, the total work of compilation, arrangement, and development of the tradition in that Gospel can with justice be viewed as the work of more than one person, perhaps even a school.

When Luke defined the intention of the διήγησιν that was compiled by πολλοί as being concerned to set forth "the things which have been fulfilled among us," his words describe one of the characteristic features of the Gospel of Matthew. For in Matthew the motif of the fulfillment of prophecy is prominent.

When Luke referred to the tradition that had been compiled by πολλοί into διήγησιν as having been "delivered to us by those who were from the beginning eyewitnesses" (Luke 1:2), he clearly associated himself with the "many" compilers, in distinction from those who were from the beginning "eyewitnesses."

The compositional character of the Gospel of Matthew reflects the results of the very process of composition that Luke describes. That is, Matthew can be justly referred to as διήγησιν,

12. See Farmer, *Synoptic Problem*, p. 4 n. 5.

made up of tradition that had been handed down from an earlier "eyewitness" period.

It is preferable, therefore, on Lessing's terms, where διήγησιν is taken to refer to a single narrative, to identify this narrative with the known Gospel of Matthew, rather than Lessing's "apostolic" Gospel of the Nazarenes, which after all is highly conjectural.

There is no doubt that from the point of view of readers who were sensitive to the prevailing standards of Hellenistic historiography, the Gospel of Matthew was defective διήγησιν. It was not set within an adequate chronological framework, so that readers acquainted with world history could view it within the context of that history. It contained duplicate accounts of certain events, and reported these as if they were completely separated in time and circumstance, when it was clear that they were but different accounts of the same matter. There were problems with the order in which certain material appeared in Matthew; thus, no sufficient reason is given for Jesus to have left Nazareth of Capernaum at the beginning of his ministry in Galilee, though a story of his being rejected by the people of his native place is included later in the narrative. And the call of the disciples after his great Sermon on the Mount, rather than before, is subject to the criticism of being anachronistic, in view of the indications that the sermon was for the disciples.

At all such points Luke's Gospel seems to reflect the results of a prolonged and careful study of Matthew, with a view to the creation of a new διήγησιν that would be free of such defects.

In addition, of course, Luke obviously had access to other material that had been compiled and handed down from the earlier period. And Schleiermacher was no doubt correct in perceiving that it was largely out of such earlier compilations of material that both Matthew and Luke were composed.[13] To what extent these briefer compilations could also have been in Luke's mind when he referred to διήγησιν having been compiled by πολλοί, remains uncertain. What is certain, however, is that Luke's Gospel is the result of careful study of the work of earlier redactors en-

---

13. *Über die Schriften des Lukas: Ein kritischer Versuch* (Berlin: Reimer, 1817); English translation, Connop Thirlwall, *A Critical Essay on the Gospel of St. Luke* (London: Taylor, 1825), containing an account of the controversy respecting the order of the first Gospels since Bishop Marsh's dissertation.

gaged in the task of producing διήγησιν. And it is quite possible
that the Gospel of Matthew was in his mind, and in the minds of
his intended readers, at the time he composed his prologue.

Step 12

Thesis: *Assuming that there is direct literary dependence between Matthew and
Luke, internal evidence indicates that the direction of dependence is that of Luke
upon Matthew.*

In support of this thesis are passages found in Matthew that
express a point of view antithetical to the mission to the Gentiles,
such as Matt. 10:5, "Go nowhere among the Gentiles," or the con-
tinuing importance of Jewish practice, such as Matt. 24:20, "Pray
that your flight may not be in the winter or on a sabbath," passages that are not found in Luke. Words and customs that would
have become increasingly less intelligible as the frontiers of the
Christian movement expanded farther and farther from its place
of origin, such as *Raca* for "fool" in Matt. 5:22, and the wearing of
phylacteries in Matt. 23:5, are not found in Luke.

The Semitic parallelism of passages in Matthew, like that in
Matthew 7:24–27, is frequently broken in the parallel passage in
Luke (cf. Luke 6:47–49). The assumption is that during the oral period, beginning with Jesus, teaching was cast in the form of
Semitic parallelism for purposes of oral communication. When
this was incorporated in a written Gospel, the possibility existed
for the writer to be conservative in editing his material, and thus to
preserve the form of Semitic parallelism. However, to do so was
not necessary for purposes of written communication, and in fact
to reproduce certain cases of parallelism in all their formal fullness
was, in some circles, to make the author's writing subject to the
criticism of redundancy. It may be assumed, therefore, that the fact
that in Luke Semitic parallelism is frequently broken, whereas in
the parallel passages in Matthew it is frequently preserved, indicates that Luke has altered Matthew and not vice versa.[14]

14. See C. F. Burney, *The Poetry of Our Lord: An Examination of the Formal
Elements of Hebrew Poetry in the Discourses of Jesus Christ* (Oxford: Clarendon,
1925), for a decisive study of the bearing of the phenomena of Semitic parallelism on the question of the original form of sayings attributed to Jesus in the

For a comprehensive and detailed up-to-date demonstration of how Luke made use of Matthew, see McNicol et al., eds., *Beyond the Q Impasse* (see *SRD*, vol. 5).

Step 13

Thesis: *The weight of external evidence is against the hypothesis that Matthew was written after Luke.*

It is not possible to settle with finality the question of the extent to which one should rely upon the unanimous testimony of the church fathers that Matthew was written before Luke. But whatever weight is to be given to this external evidence goes against the view that Matthew was written after Luke, and in favor of the view that Luke was written after Matthew.

Statements by the fathers on this matter cannot be dismissed as totally irrelevant. These fathers all came out of the apostolic church, which by the middle of the second century had formulated the canon in which Matthew and Luke were included. That church and its canon were, at least in large part, a result of the mission to the Gentiles in the apostolic period. Between Matthew and Luke, the latter was more suited for use in the Gentile churches. By comparison with Luke, Matthew retained features that were peculiarly Jewish and reflected the interests of the earlier Jewish-Christian mission (see step 12). Therefore, it is unlikely that a unanimous tradition would have developed in the Gentile church that reversed the true relationship between Matthew and Luke. That is, if Luke had been written before Matthew and had been copied by Matthew, so that Matthew then would have been a later Judaized version of Luke, it would be unlikely for a unanimous tradition to have developed among the Gentile churches that gave pride of place to Mat-

---

Gospels. Burney went beyond the evidence in suggesting that all material cast in the form of Semitic parallelism had come from Jesus. All his work actually proves is that it is possible to recover in many cases the more original form of sayings in the Gospels by studying them in the light of available knowledge of the formal characteristics of Hebrew poetry. For the purpose of settling the question of whether Luke is more likely to have altered Matthew or vice versa, however, Burney's work provides reliable criteria for a general determination of the probabilities of the matter.

thew. It is historically more probable that attributing pride of place to the more Jewish Gospel reflects a reliable historical memory in the Gentile churches as to the true chronological relationship between these two Gospels.

Step 14

Thesis: *The weight of external evidence is against the hypothesis that Matthew was written after Mark.*

The same considerations set forth in support of the thesis advanced in step 13 argue in favor of this thesis. Where the reader finds "Luke" in the discussion of step 13, he or she need only substitute "Mark," and the same conclusions that apply to the relationship of Luke to Matthew apply also to the relationship of Mark to Matthew.

Step 15

Thesis: *That Mark was written after both Matthew and Luke is in accord with the earliest and best external evidence on the question.*

Papias's testimony throws no light on the question of the order in which the Gospels were written. The earliest statement on the question of the order in which the Gospels were written is given by Clement of Alexandria, who stated that he had it from the primitive elders that the Gospels with genealogies were written before the Gospels without them.

The date of Clement's statement is uncertain, but it probably takes the investigator back to the first quarter of the second century, at which time many Christians who were active in the church when the Gospels were written were still alive. Christians in their twenties when the Gospels were written would have been in their sixties or seventies during the first quarter of the second century. This means that at the time when this tradition was formulated and passed on by those primitive elders, the primitive elders concerned had a living memory of the Gospels of Matthew and Luke being in existence before other Gospels without genealogies, such as those of Mark,

John, Peter, Thomas, the Ebionites, and Marcion. It has been suggested that in the first quarter of the second century, when this tradition was first formulated, the primitive elders were primarily concerned to set apart the later apocryphal Gospels, all of which were without genealogies. It does seem likely that some such concern was at the bottom of this tradition. However, it could not have been passed on by the primitive elders without at the same time setting apart Mark and John later than Matthew and Luke. We must bear in mind that this tradition carries us back in time to the period before the church formulated the fourfold Gospel canon. It is a tradition that appears to be free of theological bias.

For a subsequent treatment of topics covered in steps 13, 14, and 15, see "Part One: The Patristic Evidence" in *New Synoptic Studies*.[15] Note especially the article by Giuseppe Gamba, "A Further Reexamination of Evidence of Early Tradition," and the article by David Peabody, "Augustine and the Augustinian Hypothesis: A Reexamination of Augustine's Thought in *De Consensu Evangelistarum*," in which Peabody draws attention to the fact that in Book IV, Augustine distances himself from the view he gives in Book I, which nonetheless became the traditional view of the church down to the time of the Reformation, and is still so regarded today in some circles; whereas the more mature but little-known view of Augustine set forth in Book IV is supportive of the two-Gospel hypothesis in the sense that Augustine is rejecting his earlier view that Mark was a follower and abbreviator of Matthew. He now recognizes that Mark also has much in common with Luke, and in fact, according to Augustine, Mark actually unites the kingly theme of Matthew with the priestly theme of Luke. It is true that Augustine in making this point is not evidencing any direct interest in the Synoptic problem as we have come to understand it since the Enlightenment. Yet, it would be a mistake to say that what Augustine says in Book IV has no relevance for solving the question of the sequence in which those Gospels were written.

15. Ed. William R. Farmer (Macon, Ga.: Mercer University Press, 1983), 3–64 (see *SRD*, vol. 2).

It is important at this point to turn to what Augustine actually says:

> Mark, who seems to answer to the figure of the *Man* . . . either appears to be preferentially the companion of Matthew as he narrates a larger number of matters in unison with him and therein acts in due harmony with the idea of the kingly character whose want it is, as I have stated in Book I, to be not unaccompanied by attendants; or else in accordance with the more probable account of the matter he holds a course in conjunction with both. For although he agrees with Matthew in the larger number of passages, he nevertheless agrees with Luke in several others; and this very fact shows him to stand related at once to the lion and to the calf, that is to say, to the kingly office which Matthew emphasizes and the sacerdotal which Luke emphasizes.

Of course, it is conceivable that Mark could have united the kingly theme that Augustine perceives in Matthew with the priestly theme that he perceives in Luke without having known either of these Gospels. After all, these themes exist independently of the question of whether they appear respectively in these two Gospels. Peabody points out, however, that in moving toward his point that Mark has united the kingly and priestly themes of Matthew and Luke, he clearly envisions Mark as composing his Gospel with a knowledge of the work of his predecessors Matthew and Luke. This is in complete accord with the earlier tradition handed on by Clement of Alexandria. There is no evidence, however, that Augustine is being directly influenced by this earlier tradition. His shift from the view he set forth in Book I to the different view he is now setting forth in Book IV appears to be based on his own study of the texts of all three of these Gospels.

Augustine recognized the close literary relationship between the Gospels, but he also recognized that each had had distinctive features of its own. He liked to think in terms of the major themes of the Gospels. He liked to see the four canonical Gospels standing in some grand coherent christological relationship to one another, a relationship through which each complemented and supplemented the others. This was in contrast to any tendency to pit one evangelist against another or to lift up discrepancies. Augustine wanted to lift up the harmony of the four. In view of considerations like these, I agree with those who say that what Augustine says in Book IV was not said to persuade his reader to take one side or another in the modern debate between advocates of the two-source hypothesis and advocates of the two-Gospel hypothesis. However, this only serves to make what he does say all that much more important for our discussion, for what he says cannot fairly be dismissed as due to a bias one way or the other on the issue before us. The relevance of what he has written in Book IV to the issue we face is quite inadvertent.

But the conclusion that the relevance of his words for our debate is inadvertent does not diminish the importance of this relevance; on the contrary, if anything, it serves to encourage the fair-minded reader to take an ever more careful look at what Augustine actually has written in Book IV. When approached in this even-handed manner, what Professor Peabody has written on this matter will be found to be a carefully crafted report on an important discovery, a report that, in my opinion, does not overstate the case, but rather analyzes the evidence carefully and in detail, and then sets forth the relevance of this evidence for underscoring its bearing on the question of Mark's relationship to Matthew and Luke. In Book IV Augustine knows more about the Gospels than he did when he wrote Book I. In Book I he recognized that Mark, in composing his Gospel, "held a course" in conjunction with Matthew alone, but by the time he wrote Book IV, he had changed his mind. His change of mind was caused by his recognition that Mark, in composing his Gospel, "holds a course" in conjunction with "both" Matthew and Luke, not just with Matthew alone. Augustine does not out-of-hand rule out his earlier view set forth in Book I, but he contrasts that view "with the more probable account of the matter," which he now sets forth in Book IV. In balance, then, Augustine's mature, "more probable" account in Book IV, where he envisions Mark holding a course "in conjunction with both" Matthew and Luke, is in accordance with the view that supports the case for the two-Gospel hypothesis, because this hypothesis also envisions Mark following a compositional course in conjunction with both Matthew and Luke.

But—it may be argued by a careful student of the text—we have to note that there appears to be a shift in linguistic usage by Augustine that calls into question this appeal to Book IV in support of the two-Gospel hypothesis. This is because in the first option, which Augustine sets forth in Book I, where he emphasizes that Mark followed Matthew, he uses the expression *dicit* ("narrates"): Mark "narrates many things in common with Matthew"; whereas in the second option, set forth in Book IV, where Augustine envisions Mark following both Matthew and Luke, he uses a different expression: *incedit* ("walks"). Therefore, it appears possible to conjecture that when Augustine concludes that Mark "walks with both" in Book IV, he does not mean to imply that Mark narrates many things in common with "both Matthew and Luke." Following this line of reasoning, one can think that there may be some reasonable doubt as to whether Augustine envisioned a literary dependence of Mark on Luke in Book IV as he clearly did envision a literary dependence of Mark on Matthew in Book I.

This careful demurral by those who are not persuaded that Augustine in Book IV holds a view of the relationship among the Gospels that supports the two-Gospel hypothesis deserves an equally careful response by those who hold that what Augustine writes in Book IV remains, in balance, supportive of the two-Gospel hypothesis.

Let us return to the text of Augustine. We begin by noting that although Augustine's use of different expressions in referring to the relationship between Mark and Matthew alone in Book I and the relationship he envisioned between Mark and both Matthew and Luke in Book IV creates the exegetical possibility that he does not envision a literary dependence of Mark on Luke, that exegetical possibility is reduced to the logical status of "improbable" by what Augustine actually writes in the immediate context of Book IV.

What Augustine immediately by way of explanation goes on to say is this: "For, although Mark agrees with Matthew in many [or the larger number of] things, he nevertheless agrees with Luke [to a greater extent than he agrees with Matthew] in several others." In this case only one relational expression is used, *congruit*, and it is used both to express the relationship of Mark to Matthew as well as the relationship of Mark to Luke. This clearly indicates—if indeed it does not prove—that the unquestioned literary relationship Augustine has in mind in Book I is also presupposed in the argument he sets forth in Book IV. Augustine, by the time he was ready to write Book IV, had discov-

ered what he did not know when he wrote Book I: the number
of times that Mark narrates things in common with Luke, while
far fewer than the number of times he narrates things in common with Matthew, nonetheless is sufficient to indicate to Augustine that Mark followed both.

Reasonable doubt as to whether this is the more probable
way in which to interpret what Augustine has written on this
matter is further reduced by the fact that when in Book I Augustine bases his conclusion that Mark is following Matthew on the
observation that Mark narrates "many things" in common with
Matthew, so also in Book IV in similar language he argues from
this same agreement in "many things" between Mark and Matthew to the conclusion that Mark is also following Luke because
of the same kind of evidence, even if this kind of agreement between Mark and Luke is notably less.

To insist that Augustine need not necessarily be interpreted
this way is permissible. Certainly, more discussion is in order.
Meanwhile, however, it should be acknowledged that the claim
that there is a more probable interpretation of what Augustine
has written that is supportive of the two-Gospel hypothesis is
not without merit. It should also be acknowledged that this support being inadvertent does not diminish its relevance for evalu-
ating conflicting claims by advocates of alternative hypotheses
for solving the Synoptic problem.

Step 16

Thesis: *A historical-critical analysis of the Synoptic tradition, utilizing both literary-
historical and form-critical canons of criticism, supports a hypothesis that recognizes
that Matthew is in important respects secondary to the life situation of Jesus and to
the primitive Palestinian Christian community persecuted by Paul; that this Gospel
was utilized by Luke; and that Mark made use of both Matthew and Luke, and frequently combined or blended their respective texts.*

The reader can find a variety of examples of the way in which
this thesis may be supported in the criticisms of arguments for
Markan priority given in steps 3 and 4 (see especially pp. 159–
69), and the notes on the Synoptic tradition in Mark given in
step 7 (see especially pp. 265–78). How Luke made use of Mat-

thew on the two-Gospel hypothesis has been explained comprehensively and in great detail in *Beyond the Q Impasse* (see *SRD*,
vol. 5). Exactly how Mark made use of both Matthew and Luke
is presently being set forth in the forthcoming book by the same
research team that produced *Beyond the Q Impasse*. The three
canons of criticism utilized in the analysis of the Synoptic tradition referred to in this thesis are as follows:

(1) Assuming that the original events in the history of the
Christian movement took place in Palestine, within predominantly Jewish circles, and that by the time the Gospels were
written Christianity had expanded outside of Palestine and outside of circles that were predominantly Jewish in orientation:
That form of a particular tradition found in the Gospels which
reflects an extra-Palestinian or non-Jewish provenance is to be
adjudged secondary to a form of the same tradition that reflects
a Palestinian or Jewish provenance.[16]

(2) Assuming the redactional tendency to add explanatory
glosses, and otherwise to alter tradition to make it applicable to
new situations in the churches: That form of a tradition which
exhibits explanatory redactional glosses, and changes aimed to
make the tradition more applicable to the needs of the church,
is to be adjudged secondary to a form of the tradition that is free
of such redactional glosses and modification.[17]

(3) Assuming the tendency of all writers to use some words
and phrases more often than is generally true for other writers
when dealing with the same subject: That form of a tradition
which exhibits words or phrases characteristic of a redactor
whose hand is clearly traceable elsewhere in the same Gospel is
to be adjudged secondary to a form of the same tradition that is
free of such words and phrases. And, as a corollary to this: That

16. See E. P. Sanders, *The Tendencies of the Synoptic Tradition*, SNTSMS 9
(Cambridge: Cambridge University Press, 1969), 290–93 (*SRD*, vol. 1), where
several of forty-six cases he discusses where Mark is judged by advocates of the
two-source hypothesis to be secondary to either one or the other or to both of
Matthew and Luke illustrate the use of this canon of criticism.

17. See especially McNicol et al., eds., *Beyond the Q Impasse* (*SRD*, vol. 5),
for examples where the canon of "changes aimed to make the tradition more
applicable to the needs of new situations in the churches" for which Luke is
writing are cited in order to demonstrate that the text of Luke is frequently secondary to the parallel text of Matthew.

form of a tradition which exhibits words or phrases characteristic of a redactor whose hand is traceable only in another Gospel is to be adjudged secondary to the form of the parallel tradition in the Gospel where the redactor's hand can be clearly traced, provided the characteristic word or phrase occurs in the former Gospel only in passages closely paralleled in the latter, where the verbatim agreement indicates direct literary dependence.[18]

No one of these canons of criticism is decisive in any given instance. Only when they combine to reinforce one another in indicating that one particular form of a tradition is clearly secondary to another form of the same tradition can the critic with confidence render a judgment between primary and secondary material.

These canons do not exhaust all the literary and form-critical guides available to the student of the Gospels. The first canon, however, is especially inclusive and is intended to cover all such valid considerations as pertain to the presence or absence of Semitic parallelism in the formal structure of Gospel material, and the presence or absence of such literary forms as may be distinctive of the Hellenistic world.

These three canons supplement the six set forth by Ernest De Witt Burton in his monograph *Some Principles of Literary Criticism and Their Application to the Synoptic Problem.*[19] Burton stated that in questions of literary dependence between two documents, that document is to be adjudged dependent which contains features of a secondary character. The following he regarded as evidences of a secondary character:

> (1) manifest misunderstanding of what stands in one document on the part of the writer of the other; (2) insertion by one writer of material not in the other, and clearly interrupting the course of thought or symmetry of plan in the other; (3) clear omission from one document of matter which was in the other, the omission of which destroys the connection; (4) insertion of matter the motive for which can be clearly seen in the light of the author's general aim, while no motive can be discovered for its omission by the au-

18. See "Redaction Criticism and the Synoptic Problem" in *Society of Biblical Literature*, V. I, 1971 (*SRD*, vol. 1), and "Certain Results Reached by Sir John C. Hawkins . . ." in *Synoptic Studies: The Ampleforth Conferences of 1982 and 1983* (*SRD*, vol. 3).

19. Chicago: University of Chicago Press, 1904.

thor if he had had it in his source; (5) vice versa omission of matter traceable to the motive natural to the writer when the insertion (of the same matter in the other Gospel) could not thus be accounted for; (6) alterations of other kinds which conform the matter to the general method or tendency of the author.[20]

The six evidences of the secondary character of a document, outlined by Burton, together with the preceding three canons for the analysis of Synoptic tradition provide the most important guides necessary for a study of the history of the redaction of the Synoptic tradition at the hands of the canonical evangelists.[21]

Considerations that sometimes have influenced students of the Gospels in their statements about the Synoptic problem, but are either irrelevant or inconclusive and therefore have little or no probative value in settling a question of literary dependence, may be listed as follows:

(1) *The relative length of a given passage.* Since writers sometimes enlarge and sometimes condense their sources, the relative length of a given passage, by itself, offers no criteria by which it may be adjudged primary or secondary to another.

(2) *The grammar and style of a writer.* In general, since some writers improve the grammar and style of their sources while others spoil it, such considerations provide no objective basis by which one document may be adjudged primary or secondary to another. Thus, it may be said that in general there is no provable correlation between style and chronology in matters involving the question of literary dependence between documents of the same period and class of literature. If, however, it can be demonstrated that a particular grammatical usage or the usage of a particular word or phrase is characteristic of the style of a particular author, then the appearance of such a characteristic linguistic usage in another related document where the verbatim agreement is so close as to indicate copying, that closely related

20. Ibid., 198.
21. There are additional canons of criticism that must be observed when the critic attempts to trace the history of a tradition back to its beginning and to make a judgment about its probable authenticity considered as a saying of Jesus or its reliability considered as tradition about him. These, however, do not play a decisive part in the study of the Synoptic problem, and therefore are not set forth here.

document may be deemed to be literarily dependent on the one in which the linguistic usage is characteristic. And when the linguistic usage in question *never occurs* in the one document except in a passage or passages where the verbatim agreement between the two indicates copying by one author of the work of the other, but *does occur* in the other document often enough to indicate that it is characteristic of the linguistic usage of *that* author, then, but only then, can one say there is any objective grammatical or stylistic basis by which one document may be adjudged primary or secondary to another.

(3) *The Christology of a given passage.* Since the letters of Paul disclose that Christology was already both complex and highly developed in some circles in the period before the Gospels were written, and since our knowledge of christological developments in the churches in the post-Pauline period depends upon a correct solution to the problem of the chronological and literary relationship between the Gospels, and not vice versa, the Christology of a given passage in the Gospels affords the critic no reliable criteria by which to adjudge it primary or secondary to its parallel in another Gospel. Moreover, exactly how Christology developed in the period between the composition of the first of the Synoptic Gospels and the composition of the last is not known. Nor can it be assumed that in this period Christology developed in the same way, or at the same place, in the different parts of the church where the separate Gospels were respectively composed.

This is not to deny that the life situation of Jesus can be distinguished from that of the time of Paul. The tendency of the early church was to modify the tradition from Jesus in the light of the post-Easter faith in him as the risen Lord. Nonchristological statements of Jesus can therefore be distinguished from christological statements that reflect later doctrinal development following the resurrection.

But there is no reliable way in which to adjudge the Christology of Mark as earlier or later than that of Matthew or Luke. All three Gospels came from the post-Pauline period of the early church, about which very little is known apart from inferences derived from the Gospels themselves. Apart from the Gospels there is no secure basis upon which to reconstruct a scheme of christological development in this period against which to measure the relative date of a specific christological reference in the Gospels. For this reason, the Christology of a given passage offers no objective criteria by which it can be judged primary or secondary to a related Christology in a parallel passage. Nor can the omission or the insertion of such a detail offer proof of the relative primary or secondary character of a given passage, unless it be connected in some way with one of the objective canons of criticism listed above or some other valid canon of criticism.[22]

Since 1964 several new fronts have been opened up in the study of the Synoptic problem. Briefly mentioned, they are as follows:

1. the relevance of a knowledge of the philosophical schools in antiquity for understanding Mark, and the public need of the church for Gospels that were not subject to the criticism of being self-contradictory[23]
2. the relevance of a knowledge of synopsis construction for understanding the need for multicolumned synopses in understanding the interrelationships between the texts of the Synoptic Gospels[24]
3. the relevance of a knowledge of text criticism for understanding the Synoptic problem
4. the relevance of genre criticism for understanding the composition of the Gospels and their literary interrelationships
5. the relevance of knowing the social history of Gospel criticism since the Enlightenment for identifying ideological

22. For a developed and further researched treatment of this step, see William R. Farmer, *Jesus and the Gospel: Tradition, Scripture, and Canon* (Philadelphia: Fortress, 1982), parts 1 and 2, pp. 30–176. (See *SRD*, vol. 2, for part 2: "From the Gospel Tradition to the Gospel Genre.")

23. Professor David Dungan first raised this perspective as a possible way to understand Mark's composition in "Reactionary Trends in Gospel Composition: Marcion, Tatian and Mark" in *L'Évangile selon Marc: Tradition et Rédaction*, ed. M. Sabbe, BETL 34 (Leuven: Leuven University Press, 1974). He comments on it further in his *History of the Synoptic Problem: The Canon, the Text, the Composition, and the Interpretation of the Gospels*, ABRL (New York: Doubleday, 1999) in the chapters on Justin Martyr and Tatian.

24. Once again it was Professor Dungan who first opened up this front in his article on "The Theory of Synopsis Construction," *Bib* 61 (1980): 305–29. It has been a burning issue in his mind ever since.

influence upon scholarship, and in particular, the influence of civil religion on research in the German universities in the nineteenth century

6. the relevance of knowing the whole story of the development of our understanding of the problem of how our Gospels were composed, beginning with the composition of Luke's preface[25]

I close with an observation made by Hans-Herbert Stoldt. After mercilessly deconstructing every argument for Markan priority brought forth in the nineteenth century, and after having laid out in a powerful way his own case for Mark being third, he closes his book this way:

It is erroneous to believe that the study of Gospel sources can be regarded as already closed. On the contrary, it is entering a new phase, in which an altered perspective provides us with a new viewpoint and a new evaluation. And that means that in Gospel research, we do not stand at the endpoint. We stand—rather—at a turning point.[26]

Within three years of this little cloud appearing on the horizon of German criticism, Southwestern Baptist Theological Seminary hosted a "Colloquy on New Testament Studies: A Time for Reappraisal and Fresh Approaches," and invited E. P. Sanders, Helmut Koester, and David Dungan, among others, to read major papers. Helmut Koester, in his major address, laid out in detail convincing linguistic evidence that the text of canonical Mark—the only Gospel of Mark that we have—was written after the Gospels of Matthew and Luke. This little time bomb from Harvard University has yet to explode in the minds of those who still think in terms of Mark being our earliest Gospel.

In noting that the title of the symposium that generated the present volume carries the subtitle "A Time for Reappraisal," I cannot help but think that its organizers see us as standing in

25. In this connection we now have Professor David L. Dungan's monumental *History of the Synoptic Problem*.

26. *Geschichte und Kritik der Markushypothese* (Göttingen: Vandenhoeck & Ruprecht, 1977); ET, *History and Criticism of the Marcan Hypothesis*, trans. D. L. Niewyk, SNTW (Macon, Ga.: Mercer University Press, 1980), 261.

some meaningful continuity with that scholarly gathering at a sibling Baptist theological seminary twenty years ago. Since that time, the pace of research on the Synoptic problem has continued unabated. When Stoldt referred to a "turning point," I think that he was speaking prophetically, and that the turning point at which we find ourselves today is simply this: whereas, in universities, both in Europe and in the United States, Gospel research today continues to follow an agenda fundamentally shaped by the needs of civil religion, in some of our evangelical seminaries there is now the possibility, as is evidenced by the present symposium, for scholars to make a choice: will we continue to invest our time and energy in research responsive to the needs of civil religion, or are we prepared to allow our research agenda to be responsive to the needs of the living community for which the Gospels are more than literature, for which they are Scripture—Word of God?

Experts on the Synoptic problem who continue to defend the two-source hypothesis, like Neirynck of Louvain and Tuckett of Oxford, have granted in print that all the arguments of Streeter are now to be regarded as either circular or inconclusive. All experts on the Synoptic problem—and by "experts" I am referring to scholars who have published the results of their research—acknowledge that there is no convincing argument from Streeter for the priority of Mark.

The most powerful argument for Markan priority today is the argument from authority. As this argument goes, since the majority of New Testament scholars continue to adhere to this hypothesis, it should be taught to the students as being the most probable hypothesis. There are two things wrong with this argument. First, those who use it fail to make a distinction between New Testament scholars in general and New Testament scholars who have done research and have submitted their research results to peer review in learned journals or in university press publications. Among the experts on the Synoptic problem, defenders of the two-source hypothesis are no longer a majority. Ten years ago at a conference on the minor agreements held in Germany under the auspices of the Göttingen University faculty of theology, with Professor Georg Strecker as director, defenders of the two-source hypothesis were a minority. Most of the experts at that symposium defended the Deutero-Marcus hypothesis, which has the advantage of offering a better explanation for the minor agreements than can be given on the two-source hypothesis. The situation today is that the dominant critical hypothesis in Germany among scholars who are publishing work on the Synoptic problem is a Deutero-Marcus hypothesis. In England, on the other hand, the majority of scholars who are experts on the Synoptic problem—and there are not many in that fair land—adhere to the Austin Farrer hypothesis, which, while it continues to posit the priority of Mark, insists that Luke did know and use Matthew, which serves to remove the theoretical basis for belief in Q. *Beyond the Q Impasse,* published in 1996, strongly supports the Austin Farrar hypothesis on this point. On this side of the Atlantic, however, the majority of scholars publishing research on the Synoptic problem are proponents of the two-Gospel hypothesis.

A second flaw in the argument from authority is that it does not give consideration to the fact that the two-source hypothesis faces more serious difficulties than any of the other major alternatives being defended today. This fact was brought out eleven years ago by E. P. Sanders and Margaret Davies in their advanced textbook, *Studying the Synoptic Gospels.*[27]

---

27. Philadelphia: Trinity Press International, 1989.

5

RESPONSE

Grant R. Osborne

Certainly, source criticism has returned as one of the important issues in Gospel studies today. The essays in the symposium have established that beyond any doubt. The way one approaches and understands each Gospel is largely dependent on the way they relate to one another at the literary level. It makes a great deal of difference if Mark depends on Matthew, or Matthew depends on Mark, or they were independent of one another. It is the purpose of this discussion to address this issue. Two caveats are in order. First, we make no pretense of solving the issue. Our desire is to sum up the data and perhaps move the issue forward by one small step. It is likely that the problem will never be solved, at least to the satisfaction of the majority of scholars. We will not come to any consensus in this meeting. Second, my task is not to sum up the state of scholarship on the matter. Each of the essays has to a large extent done so. Therefore, I will not have the number of footnotes they have. Rather, I will provide my own perspective on the issues.

Let me give my personal history on the matter. Early in my education I was trained largely in the fundamentalist camp. I was taught that Q was accepted only by liberals and was dangerous. Topics like source criticism were to be avoided at all costs. It was not until I reached seminary that I discovered that it was a literary issue centering on the relationship of the Gospels to one another rather than a point of orthodoxy. As I began to focus more and more on redaction-critical studies in my training, I started to realize how essential it was to make a decision because the entire study of the evangelists using their sources depended to a large extent on which direction the flow of information went.

The one school of thought that has been neglected in this symposium is the independence position, which argues that there was no literary relationship between the four Gospels. I believe there are three reasons why it is largely ignored: (1) the evidence for literary dependence seems so overwhelming that it is virtually presupposed today; (2) few scholars have argued for it this century; and (3) the two major voices for the independence view in recent years, Eta Linnemann and Robert Thomas, have made it a test case for orthodoxy and vastly overstated their position. Linnemann argues largely on the basis of statistics: since there is only 46.5 percent agreement between Matthew and Mark and only 32.6 percent agreement between Mark and Luke, the agreement is more likely the result of a common oral tradition than literary dependence.[1] But there are two problems with this: (1) statistics are no better than their underlying hypotheses—if one were to allow for some redactional activity and similar rather than exact wording, the percentages would be much higher; (2) the quality of the parallels are more important than the quantity. Professor Farmer's essay has an excellent discussion (pp. 103–7) showing pericopae that have nearly exact wording (e.g., the feeding of the four thousand, Mark 8:1–10 = Matt. 15:32–39; the healing in the synagogue, Mark 1:21–28 = Luke 4:31–37; the healing of the leper, Mark 1:40–45 = Matt. 8:2–4 = Luke 5:12–16). The verbal similarities are too close to be

---

1. Eta Linnemann, *Is There a Synoptic Problem? Rethinking the Literary Dependence of the First Three Gospels*, trans. R. Yarbrough (Grand Rapids: Baker, 1992), 108.

accidental or the result of oral tradition. They demand written sources and some type of literary dependence. Moreover, the order of events in the Synoptics is too similar in places to be merely the result of chance or of oral tradition. For instance, the flashback to the death of John the Baptist, Mark 6:17–29 = Matt. 14:3–12, breaks the narrative flow of both stories and is hardly the result of tradition or accidental similarity. Also, the form of Old Testament quotations is remarkably similar in, for example, Mark 1:2 = Matt. 3:3 = Luke 3:4, or Mark 7:7 = Matt. 15:9, and that too points to some kind of dependence.[2] In conclusion, there is merit in the independence view, but insufficient evidence.[3] Literary dependence is mandated by the evidence; the only question is the direction of the flow.

Thomas argues that the independence view was the only position held for seventeen hundred years and that several scholars in the twentieth century took that approach (e.g., Thiessen, Tenney).[4] But that proves very little. It establishes precedent but not the viability of a position. The latter must be decided on its merits. No one is going to be a Calvinist because it goes back to Augustine or a dispensationalist because it goes back to Darby. However, the tradition of the independence view does demonstrate that it is worthy of inclusion in any debate. He also argues that the disagreements in the Synoptic Gospels (Matthew and Luke against Mark, Matthew and Mark against Luke, or Mark and Luke against Matthew) are merely "a random combination of agreements and disagreements that are explainable only through an independent use by each writer of tradition based on personal memories of eyewitnesses."[5] But such agreements are hardly "random," and they in fact belong more in the arguments for Markan or Matthean priority. In short, I find the inde-

2. See R. Stein, "Synoptic Problem," *DJG*, 785.

3. For others in recent years who have accepted an independence view based on the Gospels using similar oral sources, see B. Reicke, *The Roots of the Synoptic Gospels* (Philadelphia: Fortress, 1986), 181–89; R. Riesner, *Jesus als Lehrer: Eine Untersuchung zum Ursprung der Evangelien-Überlieferung*, WUNT 2.7, 3rd ed. (Tübingen: Mohr, 1988), 2–6, 512–14. See also R. Yarbrough, "Eta Linnemann: Friend or Foe of Scholarship?" *MSJ* 8, no. 2 (1997): 163–89.

4. R. Thomas and D. Farnell, eds., *The Jesus Crisis: The Inroads of Historical Criticism into Evangelical Scholarship* (Grand Rapids: Kregel, 1998).

5. Thomas and Farnell, *Jesus Crisis*, 233–46, esp. 245.

pendence view the least likely of the source-critical theories but still a possible position, and it should be represented.[6]

I will now proceed in reverse order of the presentations here, for I believe this better fits the issues.

Matthean Priority—Two-Gospel Hypothesis

Farmer has made an impressive case for Matthew being the first Gospel, with Luke using him as a source and Mark using them both. In fact, I must say, "Almost thou persuadest me!" Dungan theorizes that Matthew was written in a Palestinian Jewish-Christian environment to attest to the recently crucified Jesus, Luke during the Pauline mission to reach the Gentiles, and Mark combined Matthew and Luke in order to reconcile the Jewish and Gentile branches of the church.[7] Therefore, on the basis of Occam's razor (the simplest form of a theory is preferable), Dungan argues that it is better to choose a theory that has two simple steps than "one which invents numerous imaginary 'lost sources,' multiple 'lost versions' of the Gospels, hypothetical 'lost recensions' of Q etc. to explain the literary data."[8] Almost all New Testament scholars agree with Farmer's first four steps, that there is some type of literary dependence between the Synoptic Gospels. Of the options, the most viable are Matthean or Markan priority, although other options are possible (see the summary in Blomberg's article). Of course, there are two versions of Matthean priority: the Augustinian position, which holds that Mark used Matthew and Luke used both; and the Griesbach hypothesis, which says that Luke used Matthew and Mark used both. The latter dominates the scene today. Farmer's essay demonstrates again that the two pillars of the Griesbach, or two-Gospel, hypothesis are the phenomena of order and content and the so-called minor agreements of Matthew and Luke against Mark (p. 111). He argues strongly that of the

6. See G. R. Osborne, "Historical Criticism and the Evangelical," *Journal of the Evangelical Theological Society* 42/2 (1999), 193–210; and "Historical Criticism: A Brief Response to Robert Thomas's Other View," *Journal of the Evangelical Theological Society* 43/1 (2000), 113–17.

7. D. L. Dungan, "Two-Gospel Hypothesis," *ABD*, 6:671–72.

8. Ibid., 673.

differences between the three, the agreements of Matthew and Mark against Luke and of Luke and Mark against Matthew are far more substantial and extensive than are the agreements of Matthew and Luke against Mark. From this he concludes that Mark must have used Matthew and Luke rather than the other way around. The two-Gospel hypothesis uses each of the three areas of agreement to argue its case. When Matthew and Mark agree against Luke, it means that Luke did not follow Matthew but Mark did. When Luke and Mark agree against Matthew, it means that Mark decided to follow Luke rather than Matthew in a section where Luke went a different direction from Matthew. When Matthew and Luke agree against Mark, it means that Mark decided not to follow that tradition. In other words, the two-Gospel hypothesis is inherently coherent with its thesis.

The same is true of its argument based on the order and content of the material. Since Mark never disagrees with "the order of material common to Matthew and Luke," and since Matthew and Luke never agree in departing from the Markan order (p. 112), proponents of the Griesbach hypothesis believe it best to surmise that Mark took his order from one or the other in writing his Gospel. They argue that if Matthew or Luke were writing independently and using Mark as their primary source, it is virtually impossible that they would use Mark precisely where their order differs from each other. But if Mark were using the two as sources, it would be natural for him to choose Matthew over Luke or vice versa in places (p. 112).

Finally, the two-Gospel hypothesis believes it unnecessary to propose the hypothetical Q source, for it is more natural to suppose that the common material between Matthew and Luke was the result of Luke using Matthew as a source, perhaps one of the "eyewitnesses" of Luke 1:2. Since Luke uses many of the same techniques and a similar order as Matthew (infancy narratives, the Baptist and his teachings, the developed temptation narrative, the centrality of the Galilean ministry), there had to be some type of literary dependence between them. It is far simpler to posit dependence between Matthew and Luke than to create a hypothetical source like Q to explain the data. If the choice is between dependence and a possible series of conjectural sources, one must always choose the simpler alternative (again, Occam's razor), namely, the order Matthew-Luke-Mark over a view that embraces not only the three but also proto-Luke, Q, and possibly other sources.

Thus far the two-Gospel hypothesis sounds not only cogent but absolutely convincing. However, there are some serious drawbacks to the theory. I remember attending the 1979 Cambridge Conference on the Synoptic Gospels,[9] with several papers addressing the question "What if?" More than one presenter, upon putting forward the data on what each Gospel would look like under the Griesbach hypothesis, concluded that their study had made them more sure of Markan priority than ever. For one thing, it is difficult to explain the many omissions if Mark used both Matthew and Luke. While all of Mark can be reconstructed from Matthew and Luke, huge amounts of material would have been omitted if Mark was last. Why would he have left out the infancy narratives, the Sermon on the Mount, or all the Q material? What happened to the M and L material in his Gospel? In other words, it is easier to explain the use of Mark by Matthew and Luke than it is the use of Matthew and Luke by Mark. For instance, while Matthew and Mark have a great deal of material in common, Matthew nearly always shortens Mark rather than vice versa. This fits a key text-critical criterion: the shorter version is to be preferred.[10]

Also, while the Griesbach hypothesis can explain all the disagreements between the Gospels, it is not always so convincing on Mark/Matthew against Luke and Mark/Luke against Matthew. In a sense, this key area causes the two groups to cancel each other out. In other words, the Matthew/Luke agreements against Mark are problematic for Markan priority, but the two other sets of disagreements are problematic for Matthean priority. However, the agreements between Matthew and Luke against Mark can be explained in several viable ways. Stein notes that not only are there but few examples of such agreements, but also that "the more striking the Matthew-Luke agreements against Mark . . . the more difficult it is to explain why Mark omitted their concurrent

9. W. R. Farmer, ed. *New Synoptic Studies: The Cambridge Gospel Conference and Beyond* (Macon, Ga., Mercer University Press, 1983).

10. For an excellent application of text-critical theory to the Synoptic problem in favor of Markan priority, see M. C. Williams, "Is Matthew a Scribe? An Examination of the Text-Critical Argument for the Synoptic Problem" (Ph.D. diss., Trinity Evangelical Divinity School, 1996).

testimony; and if one seeks to explain this by stating that Mark was not bound by such concurrent testimony, one immediately raises the question of why there are not therefore many more Matthew-Luke agreements against Mark in the triple tradition."[11] In other words, this issue is problematic for both sides and fails to support either. Moreover, many feel that these disagreements are often due to an overlap between Mark and Q, to those normal differences in style that writers normally make in using sources, or to other oral tradition.[12] Professor Blomberg, in his essay, notes the significant article by Stein,[13] who points out the many instances where John agrees in wording with one of the Synoptics, but no one believes that John preceded the Synoptics. Most conclude that John is simply following a fixed tradition. A similar situation may have occasioned the Matthew/Luke agreements against Mark.

I also find the premise that Luke used Matthew a less likely reason for those sayings of Jesus common to the two than the hypothesis of a Q source (see below). The problem is the placement of the pericopae. The distribution of the similar sayings and stories in such widely divergent places and forms makes it unlikely that Luke was copying Matthew. It is far more likely that Luke and Matthew used a common source differently, in the same way that they used Mark differently.

Let me note also a few other areas where I did not find Professor Farmer's presentation convincing. First, the Griesbach hypothesis cannot provide a credible reason for why Mark was written.[14] Suggestions have moved from an apologetic desire to remove contradictions between Matthew and Luke[15] to a desire to reconcile the Jewish Gospel of Matthew to the Gentile Gospel of Luke.[16] Neither actually fits the theology of Mark or any at-

---

11. R. H. Stein, *The Synoptic Problem: An Introduction* (Grand Rapids: Baker, 1987), 136.

12. C. Blomberg, *Jesus and the Gospels* (Nashville: Broadman & Holman, 1997), 90.

13. R. H. Stein, "The Matthew-Luke Agreements against Mark: Insight from John," *CBQ* 54 (1992): 482–502.

14. Stein, *Synoptic Problem*, 133.

15. W. Farmer, "Modern Developments of Griesbach's Hypothesis," *NTS* 23 (1977): 282.

16. Dungan, "Two-Gospel Hypothesis," 672.

tempted reconstruction of a hypothetical *Sitz im Leben*. Since nearly all of Mark appears in Matthew or Luke, Mark would be doing little more than rote copying. But his Gospel is too heavily redactional and tightly written to have been little more than a compilation of Matthew and Luke. Second, the two-Gospel hypothesis makes Luke dependent almost entirely on Matthew, but the Lukan prologue mentions a multiplicity of sources (1:2). The two- or four-source theory does more justice to the data, and there is little reason why Q would not be one of those sources (see below). Finally, I must admit that of the many commentaries and monographs that have appeared over the last three decades, those from a two-Gospel perspective have seemed less persuasive to me.

Markan Priority—The Oxford Hypothesis

My preference as the title for Markan priority is B. H. Streeter's "four-source hypothesis." Not only does it separate itself more clearly from the "two-Gospel hypothesis," but it better fits the actual theory, that Matthew and Luke used not only Mark and Q but also M and L, the special material found only in their Gospels. Several of the arguments used by Streeter and his followers for this position actually do not prove much: (1) the argument from content, that 90 percent of Mark is in Matthew and 53 percent in Luke, could simply mean that Mark copied a lot from both the others; (2) the so-called eyewitness fragments in Mark, asides like Jesus "sleeping on a cushion" in 4:38 or "the green grass" in 6:39, could be seen simply as Mark's vivid style; (3) the argument from order, that Mark is the middle factor among the Synoptics, agreeing with Matthew at times and Luke at other times but never standing by himself, could point to either conclusion. These, I feel, generally support Markan priority but can be interpreted either way.

Professor McKnight centers on some of the more important arguments for the Oxford hypothesis. First, he points to the linguistic phenomena, especially the more primitive language. Mark seems more primitive and awkward in his style and content than do Matthew and Luke. This leads Matthew and Luke to "smooth out" the rough spots, for instance, when Mark emphasizes the "hardness of heart" of the disciples (6:52; 8:17) while Matthew and Luke omit that condemnation, or when Mark has Jesus say, "Why do you call me good?" (10:18) while Matthew has him say, "Why do you ask me about what is good?" (19:17 [see also the three excellent examples in McKnight's essay, pp. 84–87]). It seems more likely that Mark would use Matthew than vice versa, for it is difficult to conceive why Mark would make Matthew more clumsy. As Carson, Moo, and Morris say, this is in keeping with the text-critical principle of "the least likely reading,"[17] and McKnight asks, "Which reading most likely gave rise to the other readings?" In other words, it is more probable that Matthew smoothed out Mark than that Mark made Matthew more difficult.

I am also impressed by the argument from theological phenomena. Here also, Mark is the more difficult reading. One of the best examples is the material on discipleship failure in Mark and Matthew. Two passages will suffice: In Mark 6:51b–52, the feeding of the five thousand and the walking on the water end on a note of absolute failure when Mark comments, "They were completely amazed, for they had not understood about the loaves; their hearts were hardened." In the parallel passage, Matthew omits this, adds the story of Peter walking on the water, and concludes with their worship as they say, "Truly you are the Son of God" (14:33). It is difficult to imagine a more opposite conclusion. The same thing happens after the feeding of the four thousand, when Jesus, exasperated by their failure to understand, blasts them with his diatribe and concludes, "Do you still not understand?" (8:21). In the parallel passage, Matthew concludes with, "Then they understood" (16:12). Again, which direction more likely explains the change? Did Mark take Matthew's positive presentation of how the presence of Jesus made the difference in their failure and turn it into a diatribe against the disciples? Or did Matthew smooth out Mark's more negative theological presentation? Blomberg states unequivocally, "The major weakness in the Griesbach theory to date is that its proponents have not demonstrated how Markan style and theology emerge more consistently and coherently on their hypothesis

17. D. A. Carson, D. J. Moo, and L. Morris, *An Introduction to the New Testament* (Grand Rapids: Zondervan, 1992), 34.

than on the alternatives. Until I see such a demonstration, I will remain unconvinced" (p. 32).

Third, the redactional phenomena are another important issue. One example was given in the previous paragraph. Would Mark redact Matthew and turn it into a diatribe against the disciples? It is much more likely that Matthew made Mark more positive. Also, take Mark 6:5–6 = Matt. 13:58.[18] Mark has Jesus "unable to do any miracles except lay his hands on a few sick people and heal them," while Matthew has the simpler, "And he did not do many miracles because of their unbelief." There are two changes, Mark's "any" versus Matthew's "many," and Mark's strange addition of healing miracles in a passage that said he was powerless to perform miracles. Once more, would Mark take a plausible, straightforward statement and turn it into a difficult, seemingly inconsistent description? He certainly could have for theological reasons, but it is more likely that Matthew redacted Mark than vice versa.

Finally, a word needs to be said about M and L. L is fairly likely because in 1:2 Luke states clearly that he used more than one source in writing his Gospel. So L is a convenient symbol for those sources from which he derived those pericopae peculiar to his Gospel—for instance the infancy narratives, several stories in the travel narrative, and the Emmaus road journey. M material is more difficult, for if the tradition that it was written by the apostle Matthew is correct (as I believe), then Blomberg is correct in saying that M might well stand for "memory" (p. 29). Still, M and L are handy and probably accurate symbols for that special material. However, attempts to argue that they were individual documents like Q are singularly unconvincing.

While the above arguments certainly support Markan priority, McKnight correctly realizes that they are not absolutely conclusive. Problems still remain (we will leave the fourth difficulty, Q, for the next section). The three primary problems are well known, and there are a couple that are not as well known. First, the four-source theory is much more complex (positing Q, M, and L sources) than the two-Gospel hypothesis (which simply has the three Gospels relating to each other). Here, the text-critical criterion may well favor Matthean priority, since it is the

18. See C. M. Tuckett, "Synoptic Problem," *ABD*, 6:265.

simpler theory. Second, the evidence from the church fathers unanimously favors the priority of Matthew. However, this is also a problem for the two-Gospel hypothesis, for the fathers (apart from Clement of Alexandria) favored the order Matthew-Mark-Luke over Matthew-Luke-Mark. So technically, the patristic evidence does not favor either theory, although it is a greater problem for Markan priority. Third, the minor agreements of Matthew and Luke against Mark are problematic for the four-source hypothesis. This has already been discussed, but it must be mentioned because these agreements could point to a literary relationship between Matthew and Luke (on which see below on Q). Let me note two lesser-known problems. One is the omissions that Luke and Matthew made from Mark (e.g., the disciples' hardness of heart, the statement that Jesus' family thought he'd lost his mind [3:20–21], the seed growing secretly [4:26–29], or Luke's "Great Omission" of Mark 6:45–8:26), which has caused some to posit an *Urmarcus* that did not contain these passages.[19] But this is hardly a major difficulty, for if Mark were copying Matthew and Luke, there are even more omissions. Each of the omitted passages can be understood as redactional choices. Also, there are a couple of cases of Markan redundancy (places where Mark has duplicate expressions with Matthew having one and Luke the other), for instance:

Matthew 8:16	Mark 1:32	Luke 4:40
When evening came	When evening came and the sun had set	When the sun had set

It is said by Griesbach supporters that it is more likely that Mark collated Matthew and Luke than that they had by chance adopted different aspects of the redundancy. But Mark has many such redundant expressions (213 in all), and it seems a feature of his style more than a collation of his sources.[20]

The Q Hypothesis

The other great challenge to Markan priority has been the existence of Q. There is no mention of such a document in ancient

19. Tuckett, "Synoptic Problem," 266.
20. Ibid.

sources, and no manuscript has ever been found (though the *Gospel of Thomas* at least is a similar document). Q has been fabricated from the two- or four-source hypothesis to explain the 235 or so verses containing sayings of Jesus that are found in Matthew and Luke but not in Mark (called the double tradition). I must admit that while I have always accepted the reality of Q, I have been dubious of attempts to call it an actual document. To be honest, the speculative nature of so much that has been written about Q and the incredible variety and inventiveness of the many theories regarding its character and community have turned me off and made me wary of searching for any concrete pattern behind it. The use of it by the Jesus Seminar and others to develop a theory about Jesus as a sage and cynic philosopher rather than the crucified and risen Lord has seemed so far-fetched that I would almost retreat to a basic agnosticism about it. So in the past I tended to consider it a uniform but unwritten collection of oral traditions rather than a finished work.

However, several recent works have made me reconsider that decision. Articles such as Carlston and Norlin's analysis of the Q material,[21] have caused me to rethink the possibility that it may have been an actual document. The sayings do have a certain connected nature, and, as Blomberg says, given the prevalence of such collected wisdom sayings in the ancient world, it would be strange if the early Christians did not at some time develop such a collection of Jesus' sayings (pp. 28–29). So I am somewhat reluctantly coming to the conclusion that Q most likely was a written document, and preparing this essay has taken me further along that path, although I also agree with Professor Bock that some of the sayings in the double tradition may have come from separate oral sources, or perhaps may be separate sayings.

The primary necessity for Q comes from three conclusions: Markan priority, the presence of material common to Matthew and Luke, and the likelihood that Luke does not use Matthew. The first two have already been discussed, so let us turn to the third. The two-Gospel hypothesis, of course, argues strongly that Luke in fact does use Matthew. But does the evidence sup-

---

21. Charles E. Carlston and Dennis Norlin, "Statistics and Q—Some Further Observations," *NovT* 41 (1999): 108–23.

port this? In their infancy narratives and genealogies, there is very little connection. As Bock brings out, the Matthean discourses are often "broken up and spread across Luke rather randomly when considered from the Matthean angle" (p. 48). This rearrangement of material is difficult to explain if Luke was copying from Matthew, and the rearrangement clashes with his careful handling of Mark. For this reason, most believe that Luke has faithfully followed Q, while Matthew has collected much of it into his five discourses. Also, if Luke was utilizing the Matthean discourses, surely he would have used more of the Sermon on the Mount, mission discourse (which Stanton notes is found in seven different places in Luke[22]), or Olivet discourse. Furthermore, Luke does not use most of Matthew's additions to Mark, such as the expansive tribute to Peter as the "rock" (Matt. 16:17–19), or the exception clause in the divorce saying (Matt. 19:9). Stein goes so far as to say that Matthew's additional material to the triple tradition "is 'never' found in Luke," with only a few minor exceptions.[23] If Luke were using Matthew, these and others would probably be included.

The above material makes it unlikely that Luke was using Matthew, but that could point to independent oral traditions rather than to a common source. What makes a common source likely is another group of sayings in the double tradition (unlike those collected in Matthew's discourses) that do follow the same order. Stanton notes the following Lukan passages that "appear in Matthew in the same order: 3:7–9, 16–17; 4:1–13; 6:20b–21, 22–23, 29, 30, 32–35, 36, 37–38, 41–42, 43–44, 46, 47–49; 7:1–10, 18–23, 24–26, 27, 28, 31–34, 35."[24] This parallelism makes it unlikely that they were following independent traditions. Moreover, sayings of the double tradition have a similar theological breakdown and similar style. In fact, several have nearly identical wording (e.g., Matt. 6:24 = Luke 16:13; Matt. 11:21–23a = Luke 10:12–15). In short, Q seems to be a uniform tradition, probably a written document.

Is there any way to determine the actual contents or form of Q? Not in the way many of the so-called Q-specialists (e.g.,

22. G. Stanton, "Q," *DJG*, 647.
23. Stein, *Synoptic Problem*, 91. For exceptions, see his footnote.
24. Stanton, "Q," 645.

Mack, Kloppenberg, Jacobson, Robinson) are taking it. To seek to determine a Q community or a *Sitz im Leben* or a history of tradition for such a hypothetical document is too fanciful to undertake with any likelihood of success. This becomes downright offensive when some try to describe a Q community that does not know a messianic Jesus or a suffering Redeemer. What can be done, however, is to study Q as found in Matthew and Luke. Decisions regarding original form are as difficult in the double tradition as they are in the triple tradition, for redaction can go many different directions. It is relatively simple to suggest the primary themes and types. Bock suggests three main themes (introducing Jesus alongside John, mission and wisdom exhortation for disciples, and eschatology) and several main groups (the Baptist and Jesus, Jesus and his disciples, possibly Jesus and his opponents, practical aphorisms, and the future) (pp. 52–55). Beyond this we cannot go, but we can see real value in the sayings source named Q.

Conclusion

There are no certainties in life. It must be said that scholarship, like all other earthly endeavors, runs in fads, especially in the post-Enlightenment setting. Scholars are essentially Athenians at heart, always searching for some new thing (Acts 17:21). The four-source hypothesis has dominated for almost a century now, and that is a fairly long time. So we can never know when some new genius will come along and establish a new theory that will carry the day. However, it is the purpose of symposia like this to sum up the "state of the art" on this issue, and I believe we have done as well as we can. It seems to me that the evidence points clearly to the modified Streeter theory that Mark was first, and that it existed alongside a sayings source that we now call Q. Later, Matthew utilized both and supplemented them with his own (M)emory material. At the same time (it is nearly impossible to know which was first), Luke used Mark and Q along with other sources he had gathered (L), and wrote his Gospel. Again, certainty is impossible, and it is good for us to be "iron sharpening iron" as we debate the proper approach to interpreting the Gospels on the basis of the sources they used (redaction and composition criticism). The only mandate for all of us is humility. We need each other, for without these challenges we become arrogant and falsely certain of our community-shaped theories.

Finally, I must agree with and second McKnight's clarion call for unity among all of us against postmodernists—namely, the narrative critics and the deconstructionists. The lack of concern with history, the disregard for truth, and the switch from meaning to creative writing will eventually erode the entire purpose for scholarship as we know it. Derrida says correctly that his primary goal is to deconstruct Western epistemology and metaphysics. The one thing we are desperately concerned with is the search for truth: what really happened in the development of the four Gospels and how that can help us understand what God inspired the four evangelists to say. That is our true concern.

SUBJECT INDEX

SCRIPTURE INDEX